2000

Life In The Time Of
PERICLES AND THE ANCIENT GREEKS

LIFE IN THE TIME OF
PERICLES AND THE ANCIENT GREEKS

Michael Poulton

Illustration by John James

CHERRYTREE BOOKS

COVER ILLUSTRATIONS:

A long procession of Athenian men and youths climb up to the rebuilt Acropolis with sacrificial animals, gifts and libations for the gods.

DEDICATION:

For Blob Hands

PHOTO CREDITS:

The Art Museum, Princeton University: 31
British Museum: 11, 13, 36, 58, 59
Cassady, Richard: 44
Chang, Heidi: 54
Connolly, Peter: 15
Hook, Richard: 51
Hunt, John: 6 top, 7, 18, 41
The Louvre, Paris: 14
Martin-von-Wagner, Wurzburg, Germany: 32
Museo Arch, Naz de Ferrara: 29
Museum für Vor-und Frühgeschiche, Frankfurt: 12
Parzych, C: 25, 33
Wadsworth Atheneum, Hartford, CT. J. Pierpont Morgan Collection: 19

A Cherrytree Book

First published 1992
by Cherrytree Press Ltd
a subsidiary of
The Chivers Company Ltd
Windsor Bridge Road
Bath, Avon BA2 3AX

A Mirabel Book
Produced by Cynthia Parzych Publishing, Inc.
648 Broadway, N.Y., N.Y. 10012
Edited by: John Gilbert

Copyright © Mirabel Books Ltd 1992

British Library Cataloguing in Publcation Data
Poulton, Michael
    Pericles and the Ancient Greeks. – (Life
    in the Time of Series)
    I. Title II. Series
    938

    ISBN 0-7451-5193-0

Printed and bound in Belgium
by Proost International Book Production

Contents

1 The City-States and the Persian Wars 6

2 Marathon. 10

3 Preparations for War. 16

4 Thermopylae and Salamis 19

5 Religion 25

6 The Theatre. 31

7 The Olympic Games. 38

8 Pericles and Democracy 44

9 The Early Days of Pericles. 46

10 The Delian League. 48

11 Rebuilding Athens 50

12 Living in Athens. 52

13 The Athenian Family 55

14 The End of Pericles 60

Glossary 62

Index 63

CHAPTER 1

The City-States and the Persian Wars

About 5,000 years ago the city of Knossos on the Aegean island of Crete was one of the most prosperous trading centres in the world. Its ships carried oil, wine, grain, bronze weapons and pottery to and from other islands and towns on the western and eastern mainlands around the Aegean Sea.

Knossos dominated the Aegean Sea for many years. Its religion, myths and legends must also have travelled to distant lands, along with the trade goods that provided its riches. But by 1450 B.C., Crete's power had shifted to a group of cities on the western mainland, chief of which was Mycenae. It was the Bronze Age people of this and other cities, sometimes called ACHAEANS, who, in about 1200 B.C., sailed across the 'wine dark sea' to besiege the

The Lion Gate of the citadel at Mycenae, capital of the Achaean king, Agamemnon, who sacked the city of Troy.

walled city of Troy.

In the age before writing, the legend of the Trojan war was passed on by word of mouth. The story was first set down 400 years later in the *Iliad*, an epic poem ascribed to the blind poet Homer (who may or may not have existed). Because we know so little about what happened to the cities of the Aegean thereafter, we call the period after the fall of Troy the Dark Ages.

Historians have two conflicting ideas as to what may have occurred during those years. The first version says that at the end of the Bronze Age, the mighty Achaean city-states known to us from Homer – Mycenae, Tiryns, Sparta, Pylos, Thebes and Argos – were invaded by DORIANS, a northern people who claimed to be descended from the hero and god, Herakles (whom the Romans later called Hercules). They had iron spears and swords and gradually overran most of the mainland. The small and unimportant town of Athens seems to have escaped, perhaps buying off the invader. Sparta became the new Dorian capital, and its inhabitants had to slave for their harsh new masters. The Achaean peoples, including the IONIAN and AEOLIAN tribes, fled

Eastern Mediterranean at 450 B.C.

BLACK SEA
MACEDONIA
THRACE
ITALY
GREECE LYDIA
AEGEAN SEA
SYRIA
Rhodes
Sicily
Cyprus PERSIA
Crete
MEDITERRANEAN SEA
☐ Greek areas
miles
0   250
0   250
km
EGYPT

LEFT: Map of the eastern Mediterranean and Middle East at the time of Pericles.
RIGHT: The ruins of Sparta. Excavations have revealed temples, human and animal figures in bronze, ivory and bone, and painted pottery.

to the islands of the Aegean and to the eastern mainland, where they set up new towns and colonies.

The second version tells how these same Achaean cities quarrelled and fought with their neighbours. Those with the new iron weapons were the most successful. Sometimes towns became over-populated and founded new colonies on the Aegean islands and the eastern mainland. Athens gradually absorbed its weaker neighbours until it dominated the whole mainland area known as Attica. Sparta became the most powerful military force on the western mainland.

We do not know which, if either, of these versions is true or even partially true. Our knowledge of the history of the city-states between 1100 and 800 B.C. remains confused, a mixture of myth, legend and propaganda.

THE PERSIAN EMPIRE

Athens and the other city-states were soon compelled to meet the challenge of a great military power from the east – the empire of Persia. Ancient peoples thought that the Persians were descended from Perseus, who, according to myth, cut off the head of a terrible monster, the Gorgon, Medusa, and used it to turn his enemies into stone. The rise of Persia – modern-day Iran – was rapid and spectacular. In less than fifty years the Persians had taken over the crumbling empire of Assyria, conquered Lydia

– ruled by the enormously wealthy Croesus – and crushed Egypt. In 521 B.C. a new Persian leader, Darius, took the throne. He styled himself 'Great King', 'King of Kings' or 'King of the World'. This is his own description of how he treated one of his enemies:

When he was brought before me, I cut off his nose, ears and tongue and knocked out one of his eyes. I kept him chained up at the entrance to my palace; everybody came to look at him. Later, in Ecbatana, I impaled him. Then I took his chief supporters from the fortress at Ecbatana, flayed them all and hung up their skins.

Darius decided to push his rule even farther westwards. His armies reached the borders of Thrace, conquered or subdued the Ionian and Aeolian city-states on the eastern mainland, and overran the more powerful Aegean islands. The rulers of some city-states had to live as unwilling guests, or hostages, in Darius's court. It seemed likely that the western mainland would soon suffer the same fate.

THE ISLAND AND CITY-STATES

There were perhaps 150 states on the western mainland, each a market town surrounded by farmland. Some were quite big; Sparta and Athens counted their populations in thousands and eventually in tens of thousands.

Achaea and its City-States

ABOVE: *Map of the Achaean city-states during the so-called Dark Ages.*
BELOW: *Histiaeus tattooing the head of his slave.*

Because of the mountainous terrain, states seldom communicated with one another except during religious festivals and in times of war. The island states were better placed. The Aegean is dotted with islands, some of them quite big, like Rhodes and Crete, but others no more than a few miles wide. The seaways usually provided easier travel than the rocky roads and tracks of the mainland. Communications between the islands were fairly good except at those times of year when bad weather made sea travel risky. Sailors always liked to keep within sight of the shore.

Originally, most city-states had a royal family. Athens threw out its kings or TYRANTS, and set up what has been described as the world's first democracy. The word 'democracy' comes from two Greek words, *demos*, 'people', and *kratos*, 'power, authority', and means 'government by the people'.

The eastern mainland – today part of Turkey – had been colonized mainly from the western mainland by the Ionians and Aeolians. There were also Ionian trading posts all around the Black Sea. Grain from Ukraine was a vital import for many of the western city-states. Later there were colonies or trading communities all over the Aegean and as far away as Sicily, Italy, France, Spain, Egypt, Syria and Russia.

THE IONIAN REVOLT

One reluctant guest at the court of Darius was Histiaeus, ruler of the Ionian state of Miletus. In 499 B.C. he organized a revolt against the Persians, knowing that, because Darius trusted him, he would be sent back to put down the uprising. Once free, he could lead it. Histiaeus summoned a trusted slave and a barber. He made the barber shave the slave's head. Then he tattooed on it a message to his son-in-law and deputy back in Miletus. The slave set off as soon as his hair had regrown. The message told the people of Miletus to start planning a revolt and to get help from the powerful cities on the western mainland. Without control of the seas Persia would be unable to supply its huge armies. Histiaeus was sure that Sparta and Athens would realize that, if they did not join together, sooner or later Darius would conquer them.

Sparta refused to help, but Athens sent twenty ships to assist Miletus and Eretria sent five. The expedition sailed to Ephesus and marched to the town of Sardis, where there was a strong Persian garrison. Sardis was sacked and burned.

The historian Herodotus tells a story of Darius when he heard of the event:

'Who are the Athenians?' he asked. When told, he sent for his bow, fitted an arrow to the string and shot it towards the sky, saying, as it rose to the heavens, 'Ruler of all gods, grant that I may one day be revenged upon the Athenians!' He then ordered one of his staff to say to him three times a day before meals, 'Lord, remember the Athenians!'

By the autumn of 498 B.C., the Persians had regrouped. They gave the rebels a severe drubbing at Ephesus. But by now other states were determined to make a last-ditch effort against the all-conquering Persians. Inspired by the example of Athens, revolts broke out in many of the subject city-states. At this point, however, the Athenians decided to go home.

It took the Persians years to stamp out the revolt. Eventually, Miletus was destroyed and its people enslaved. The Ionian fleet was divided by squabbles, laziness and petty jealousies. At Lade, in the summer of 495 B.C., the Persian navy attacked and defeated the Ionian ships. The revolt was over. Histiaeus was impaled. His head was cut off and sent to Darius.

The Persian king, Darius, swears revenge on the Athenians after the sacking of Sardis.

CHAPTER 2

Marathon

Darius, the Great King, must have become more and more irritated by being reminded of the Athenians every time he sat down to a meal. In 490 B.C. he sent an army to punish the two western states that had joined the Ionian revolt. His fleet consisted of ships from the cities and nations the Persians had conquered. Many were vessels supplied by the Ionians and Aeolians. Hippias, a member of the family who had ruled Athens before it became a democracy, accompanied the Persian army. He still had some support in Athens. Darius believed that other towns in Attica, which did

not want to see Athens become too powerful, would back Hippias. In fact, many cities on the western mainland thought that the best way to deal with the Persians was to pay them 'protection money' and hope that they would be left alone.

The Persian fleet sailed across the Aegean, stopping to burn towns, enslave adult inhabitants, and take children hostage. The people of Eretria could not decide whether to surrender or defend themselves. Athens brought help, but the Eretrians refused it, sent the soldiers home, and gave in to the Persians without a fight. Then, when the Persian army landed, they decided to resist the invaders. After seven days the city fell. Its temples were

Philippides begs for military aid from the two kings of Sparta and their council of elders.

plundered and burned, and the people were deported as slaves.

It was probably Hippias who advised the Persians to choose Marathon, about 40 kilometres northeast of Athens, for a landing. A more obvious place was the bay of Phaleron, just south of Athens. But Hippias weighed both the advantages and disadvantages. He himself had defeated a Spartan army that had tried to land at Phaleron; and his father had once launched a successful attack on Athens after landing at Marathon. The plain of Marathon was well suited to a cavalry battle, and the Persians were pinning great hopes on their mounted troops. We do not know how many Persians made their unopposed landing in the bay of Marathon, but our best estimate is between 20,000 and 25,000 men.

The Athenians had two choices: either to defend their city or go to Marathon and fight. Ten thousand HOPLITES – the heavy infantry of the city-states – marched north to meet the Persians, and a runner, Philippides (or Pheidippides) was sent to Sparta to call on its powerful army for help. He covered the distance in a single day. But the Spartans were celebrating a festival of Apollo and could not fight until the next full moon, six days later. They promised to march north and fight the Persians when the festival was over. Philippides ran back next day to Athens with the reply. Today the Spartan response might seem like an excuse or a delaying tactic. In fact, it shows how seriously the people of these times took their religion. The need to keep the support of the gods took precedence over everything. The Athenians accepted the Spartan delay as unfortunate but unavoidable. They promptly dispatched Philippides to Marathon.

THE EVE OF BATTLE

The Persian cavalry controlled the Marathon plain. Their infantry, supported by archers, took up position in front of marshland to the east. The Athenians formed up outside the town of Marathon and waited. But they could

Pottery vase depicting a hoplite saying goodbye to his family as he sets off for war.

not decide what to do next. Their army was under the command of no fewer than ten generals. Five of them wanted to wait for the Spartans. Five others, led by Miltiades, favoured an attack. The deciding vote was given to a wise and respected general named Callimachus. Miltiades cornered Callimachus before he spoke to the council of generals and persuaded him to vote for an immediate attack.

It is a wonder that the Athenians managed to make even the simplest of military decisions. Now that they had decided to go on the offensive, the army regulations said that each of the generals should command the army in turn for a day at a time. In this case, the regulations were 'bent'. Four of the generals handed over their day's command to Miltiades, who gained absolute control of the army for half the time.

The town of Plataea, which had close and friendly links with Athens, sent 1,000 soldiers to help out. Apart from this welcome gesture, the Athenians were on their own. Their problem was that, as long as the Persian cavalry dominated the plain, they could not get near the enemy infantry. The two armies were thus kept about a kilometre apart.

One night some Ionian soldiers, who had been forced to serve in the Persian ranks, deserted. They crept up to the stockade the Athenians had built and announced that the Persian cavalry were not in camp. Perhaps

they had wandered off to find food and water for their horses. Some modern historians have suggested that the Persians had changed their minds and that the cavalry were already back on board ship for a fresh landing at Phaleron. Others argue that, if the Persians had decided to quit Marathon and sail direct to Athens, the infantry would have embarked first, leaving the cavalry to protect them. But since it is a more difficult operation to embark horses than men, the Persian commanders may have considered the loss of a few thousand foot soldiers – and foreigners at that – not to be as important as ensuring the safety of their crack troops and horses. In any event, we do not know what really happened.

THE ATHENIAN VICTORY

Miltiades, who was in charge that day, acted at once. He asked Callimachus to sacrifice to the gods in order to discover the chances of success. Callimachus read the omens by examining the entrails of the slaughtered

ABOVE: Pottery vase showing Athenians sacrificing to Apollo.

TOP: The Athenian infantry pursue the Persian cavalry into the sea after the victory at Marathon.

animal. The gods seemed to be saying that the time was ripe for a sudden attack. At dawn the thin Athenian line, supported by the Plataeans, began to advance. When they came within range of the enemy arrows, they broke into a sprint and threw themselves at the Persian infantry. The Persians smashed through

the centre of the line but were encircled by the Athenian soldiers on either wing. By the time the Persian cavalry arrived, the battle had turned into a rout. The Persians ran for their lives, with the Athenians in hot pursuit. The Persians managed to scramble onto their ships, although seven could not be launched in time and had to be abandoned. One story says that Philippides was sent to carry the news to Athens. He ran all the way, gasped out 'victory', and dropped dead from exhaustion.

The Athenians began to strip the dead of their armour and to collect the spoils the Persians had left behind. As they celebrated their victory, however, they noticed that somebody in the hills to their rear was signalling to the Persian fleet, using a polished shield to reflect the sunlight and flash a message to try again. The Persians set sail, determined to do just that. This time they planned to attack Athens from the south. Miltiades immediately marched his men back to the city. It must have taken about seven hours. By the time the first Persian ships sailed into the bay of Phaleron, the

Athenians had already taken up a position in the Precinct of Herakles, south of the city walls. The Persians adopted the only sensible course of action. They sailed for home.

On the following day the Spartan advance guard of 2,000 men arrived at Marathon. They marched to the site of the battle and

Detail of the marble frieze from the Parthenon commemorating the young soldiers of Athens who died at Marathon.

celebrated temple – the Parthenon. Around the walls would be carved a marble procession of 192 Athenian youths in memory of those who gave their lives to defend the city.

Marathon was a famous victory but not the biggest, nor the bloodiest, nor even the most decisive battle of the Persian wars. Yet the Athenians were particularly proud of it, perhaps because, apart from the 1,000 Plataeans, they had stood alone against the first Persian army to land on the western mainland and defeated it. It is remembered, too, because it has a long-distance race named after it, in memory of Philippides' remarkable run to announce the Athenian victory.

Darius realized that his fleet was too weak to defeat the hated enemy. If Athens and the

helped count the dead. The Athenians had lost 192 men, the Persians about 6,400. The dead Athenians were buried together under a mound on the battlefield. (It was recently excavated, revealing the remains.) At the time of the battle, a little boy named Pericles was living in Athens. Many years later he would plan to build what became the world's most

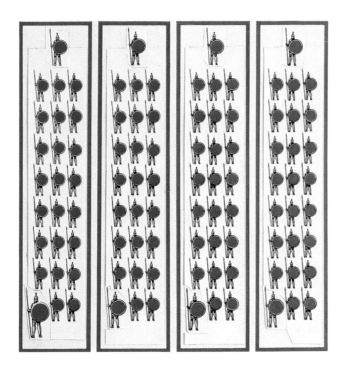

ABOVE: Diagram of a lochos, or PHALANX, the military unit made up of four groups of twenty-four hoplites and a rear guard.
RIGHT: An Athenian boy soldier dressed in cloak and sunhat, and carrying the hoplite spear that will later be his main weapon in battle.

first year, he received his own spear and shield and took the oath of loyalty at the shrine of the goddess Agraulos on the ACROPOLIS:

> 'I shall not disgrace my sacred weapons nor desert the comrade who fights at my side. I shall defend both sacred and secular things. I shall not allow the fatherland to be reduced in extent but will fight to extend and strengthen its borders. . . .'

For the next year, the boy might serve in a border garrison and take part in religious festivals. At the age of nineteen, he was liable for service in the Athenian army, as were all males up to the age of fifty-nine. The core of the army consisted of the heavily armed hoplites. These infantry soldiers were drawn from the wealthier families who could afford to pay for the necessary armour and weapons.

rest of the western mainland was to be conquered, his army would have to take an overland route. He therefore began to assemble the biggest land force the world had ever seen. But the campaign against Athens had to be postponed because of a revolt in Egypt. At this point, in 486 B.C., Darius died. His son, Xerxes, quickly quashed the Egyptian uprising and began to prepare for war with Athens.

AN ATHENIAN SOLDIER

A boy from Athens usually joined the army at the age of seventeen and would spend about two years in military training. The newly recruited teenager, or EPHEBOS, was issued with a cloak and a wide-brimmed sunhat. In the barracks he would be taught to fight with bow-and-arrow, sword, javelin and catapult. He would also learn to use the heavy hoplite spear, the main infantry weapon. Only if his spear broke in battle would he resort to the sword. At the end of the

CHAPTER 3

Preparations for War

ABOVE: Silver coins of Caulonia, with an image of Apollo on either side.
RIGHT: Athenians consulting the oracle of Apollo at Delphi. The god's wishes and advice are conveyed by the Pythian priestess who sits outside her cave.

Although in theory Athenian democracy gave all social classes (except slaves and women) a share in government, one of its weaknesses was that ordinary people could easily be swayed by a good speaker. A wily politician could stir up the feelings of a large crowd. The highest authority in Athens, the ASSEMBLY, was a meeting open to any citizen over the age of eighteen. With no time for reflection, people tended to believe the last thing they had been told. An honest politician might falter for words and fail to get his message across clearly, and thus a hard-won reputation could be shattered in a moment.

THE REMOVAL OF MILTIADES

One victim of Athenian democratic fickleness was Miltiades, the hero of Marathon. After the Persian withdrawal, an Athenian fleet commanded by Miltiades was sent to punish some of the Aegean island states that had been forced to aid the Persians. Paros was one. Miltiades tried to fine Paros 100 talents. It is difficult to say how much a talent was worth, but one talent would have paid all the expenses of a large warship and its crew for several weeks. The Parians refused to pay. Miltiades besieged their city for about a month. Then he decided that the enterprise was not worth its costs and sailed home. Back in Athens, politicians jealous of Miltiades' growing popularity used this failure to destroy him.

Badly wounded at the siege of Paros, Miltiades was brought into the Assembly, too sick to defend himself. His accuser, Xanthippus, had connections with a number of rich and powerful families. Some of these families were believed to have been in league with the Persians and even responsible for the signalling shield after the battle of Marathon. Xanthippus and his supporters must have seen the people's disappointment at Miltiades' failure at Paros. It was their chance to regain some popularity at his expense. It was said that Miltiades was the leader of 'the better people in Athens' and that Xanthippus was the leader of 'the people'. It is likely that Xanthippus's faction had packed the Assembly with country people who could be relied upon to vote as they were told.

The paint was hardly dry on the heroic picture of Miltiades in the covered meeting place in Athens known as the Painted Stoa when the Assembly found him guilty of 'deception of the people'. Xanthippus demanded the death penalty. Instead, Miltiades was fined fifty talents. He died of his wounds a few days later. Years afterwards, his son, Cimon, managed to pay off the huge debt. In Athens Miltiades was remembered by many as an honest and noble soldier who had fallen foul of an unscrupulous politician. Ironically, history

would repeat itself. Cimon was later prosecuted by Xanthippus's son, Pericles.

THEMISTOCLES

When the Athenians had finished congratulating themselves on destroying the hero of Marathon, they realized that they needed a strong war leader to replace him. Everybody knew that the Persians would soon try to invade again. After a short political struggle, they chose Themistocles. He was a self-made man without influence among the nobility. He firmly believed that the state's future lay at sea. Athens could never rival Persia or Sparta on land, but with the strongest fleet in the Aegean it could dominate the western world. In 482 B.C. a rich new vein of silver was discovered at the mines of Laurium. The Assembly recommended that the immense income

from this new mine should be shared among the citizens. Themistocles pointed out, however, that an enemy could simply march in and confiscate it. He persuaded the Athenians to spend the money on building 100 new warships and modernizing the 100 ships they already had.

As Xerxes was about to invade the western mainland, the city-states asked Sparta to lead an alliance for their defence. Sparta agreed and invited all the mainland states and many of the colonies to join. Money and soldiers would be needed to fight the Persians.

CONSULTING THE ORACLE

At this point some of the states decided to ask the gods what they should do. The god who could answer their questions was Apollo, the mouthpiece of Zeus, chief of the gods. It is

17

The foundations and a few columns are the only survivors of the ancient Temple of Apollo at Delphi, which was destroyed by an earthquake in 373 B.C.

and treasuries to receive the various gifts to the god. But, despite the buildings and activity, it was still one of the holiest places in the world.

Apollo's ORACLE could only be consulted about nine times a year. A priestess called the Pythia, after bathing in the sacred spring, would sit in a cave on a golden tripod, chewing laurel leaves. More laurel leaves were burned all around her. The person who wanted to ask Apollo either a verbal or written question would first bathe in the spring, then approach the Pythia. After working herself into a trance, she would answer the question. Sometimes the reply was straightforward, sometimes it seemed like a riddle. It was up to the many priests of Apollo to explain the Pythia's answer.

On this occasion the representatives of Sparta asked how the war would go for them. They were told to expect one of two disasters: either their town would be destroyed or one of their ruling kings would be killed. The town of Argos inquired if it should join the alliance against Persia. The answer was that it should 'sit with its spears sharpened and be ready to guard its head'. When the envoys of Athens entered the sanctuary, the Pythia told them the best thing they could do would be to run away as far as possible. Their city would be destroyed by fire and by Ares, the god of war.

The Athenians were well known as an argumentative people. Not only were they prepared to bicker with Apollo, they were even ready to try to blackmail him. They said that, if the god could not come up with a better answer, they would starve themselves to death in his sanctuary. The holy site would thus be defiled and have to be purified and reconsecrated, thereby causing great inconvenience and expense to the people of Delphi. However much Apollo might have been tempted to strike them dead, he must have resolved to give them a more hopeful reply. He told them a number of things. First, a wooden wall would protect the Athenians. Second, they should not wait for the enemy to attack them; they should retreat. Third, a day would come for fighting the enemy at Salamis but a lot of people were going to die in the conflict.

difficult to imagine the familiar terms on which the people of these times lived with their gods. For most of them, Apollo was real: he moved among them, and although few would claim ever to have seen or touched him, everyone had seen his statues. They prayed to him, flattered him or even tried to bribe him. Priests informed the people what pleased or displeased the god. The citizens of Athens 2,500 years ago believed in Apollo with fervour and dedication.

Apollo was believed to have lived at Delphi since prehistoric times. The deep chasms, the sacred groves, and the springs in the wild landscape had been overlaid with shrines, temples

CHAPTER 4

Thermopylae and Salamis

By 480 B.C. Xerxes had recruited a vast army from all over his empire. The eminent historian Herodotus described it leaving Sardis on its mission to destroy the joint forces of the Spartan alliance. His guess that it comprised 5,000,000 men is clearly too large. Modern estimates suggest between 200,000 and 250,000.

As Xerxes marched down the mainland coast, the great army was shadowed by his enormous fleet. He probably had about 1,200 triremes, manned mostly by Phoenicians, Egyptians and Cypriots. Some 300 of these ships had been taken from the Ionian states after the revolt. There were also smaller vessels designed for boarding rather than ramming. The entire Persian fleet probably consisted of as many as 3,000 ships.

THE PASS OF THERMOPYLAE

While the allied fleet awaited the Persians off Artemisium, the Spartan king, Leonidas, decided to block the enemy advance at Thermopylae, a narrow pass named after the local hot springs. The pass was about six kilometres long and nowhere more than 15 metres wide. To the right was the sea, to the left the mountains. It would have been

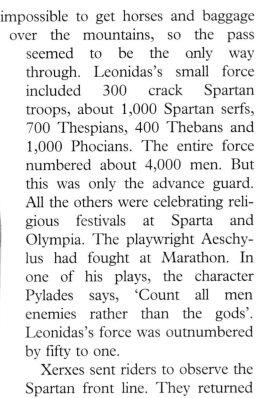

Bronze statuette of a Spartan armed for battle, with crested helmet and military cloak.

impossible to get horses and baggage over the mountains, so the pass seemed to be the only way through. Leonidas's small force included 300 crack Spartan troops, about 1,000 Spartan serfs, 700 Thespians, 400 Thebans and 1,000 Phocians. The entire force numbered about 4,000 men. But this was only the advance guard. All the others were celebrating religious festivals at Sparta and Olympia. The playwright Aeschylus had fought at Marathon. In one of his plays, the character Pylades says, 'Count all men enemies rather than the gods'. Leonidas's force was outnumbered by fifty to one.

Xerxes sent riders to observe the Spartan front line. They returned puzzled, reporting that the Spartans were either doing exercises or combing their hair. Xerxes was astonished. He summoned a Spartan traitor who had gone into exile at the Persian court and asked him why his former friends seemed so carefree. The answer came that this was how Spartans behaved when they were preparing to fight to the death.

Xerxes gave the order to attack. The pass was too narrow to use cavalry, so the infantry advanced first. But they made no impression upon the allies. Even the crack troops known as the

Immortals failed miserably. Hundreds of them were cut down. The following day went no better for the Persians.

At the end of the second day, Ephialtes, a shepherd from the town of Malis, offered to show Xerxes another pass through the mountains in return for a large reward. Leonidas already knew about this path and had sent his Phocians up to defend it. But Ephialtes led the Persian commander Hydarnes and the Immortals up the mountain track in the darkness of night. At the top they surprised the Phocians, who were driven back by showers of arrows. With their backs against the mountain slopes, they prepared for a last-ditch

The Persian king, Xerxes, leaves Sardis with his army. Horses draw the chariots that bear the king and the statue of the god Mazda.

fight. The Immortals ignored them and simply walked on down the pass.

The following morning Leonidas saw that the Persians had crossed the mountain. He would now be attacked from behind as well as from the front. He dismissed everybody except the Thebans and his 300 Spartans, telling them to retreat and live to fight another day. The 700 Thespians refused to obey the order, electing to stay and die with Leonidas.

When all seemed lost, Leonidas pulled back

from the gap and positioned his men on a small hill. The exact place has been identified by modern archaeologists who excavated the hill and found hundreds of Persian arrowheads. We are told that thousands of Persians died in attack after attack. The bodies lay so thick on the ground that they almost formed a defensive wall in front of the Spartans. Herodotus says that the Persians had to be driven towards Leonidas's men with whips. Eventually, the Spartans' spears began to break, and they were forced to fight with their swords. When Leonidas was killed, there was a furious struggle over his body. Three times the Persians tried to drag it behind their lines:

three times the Spartans dragged it back. When their swords broke, too, the Spartans continued to battle with their hands and teeth. Two Spartans had been suffering from a disease which caused a temporary blindness. One of them made his way back home and lived for a while in disgrace. The other got his slave to lead him to the battlefield where he fought blindly until he was cut down.

The Spartans were not loyally supported by all their allies. At the critical point of the battle, some of the Thebans disgraced themselves by putting their hands in the air and shouting, 'We surrender!' They claimed that they had never wanted to fight in the first place and that they were really admirers of the Persians.

Xerxes had Leonidas's head cut off and his body stripped and crucified. The Thebans were branded. This 'King of Kings' was clearly as cruel and vengeful as his father. He had lost about 20,000 men. Approximately half his fleet had been sunk or badly damaged, mainly by storms. In addition he began to realize just how difficult it would be to keep such a huge army fed and watered for any length of time.

The Spartans put a price on the head of the traitor Ephialtes, who had led the Immortals over the mountain path. He went into hiding for many years. When he thought it was safe, he returned to his own town and was immediately killed.

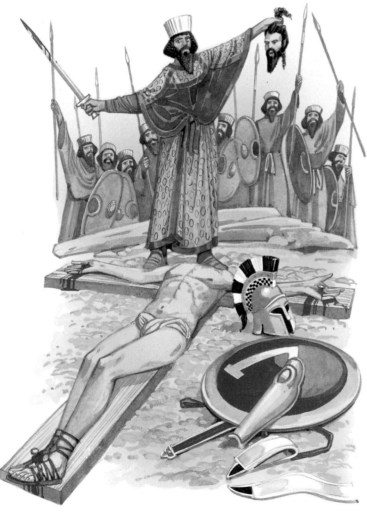

In a dishonourable act of vengeance, the body of the hero of Thermopylae, Leonidas, is crucified and decapitated by Xerxes.

THE SACK OF THE ACROPOLIS

Xerxes pushed south into Attica, plundering and burning the towns, temples and fields of his enemies. A troop of Persian soldiers was sent to Delphi. The Delphians went into Apollo's sanctuary and asked the god what they should do. Apollo told them that he would look after himself. As the file of soldiers passed under the towering cliffs near the sacred spring, a sudden storm shattered the oppressive silence. Lightning smashed the rocks on the cliff side which crashed down, killing some Persians. The rest ran away.

Athens was not so lucky. The citizens were evacuated to the island of Salamis and other nearby islands. Very old people, the sick and household pets were left behind. There is a sentimental story of Pericles' father, Xanthippus, who had a faithful dog. Sad at being abandoned, the dog jumped into the sea, swam after Xanthippus's ship, and died from the effort as it reached the shore. The dog was buried on the spot and hundreds of years later tourists were still being shown its tomb. If nothing else, the tale shows how dangerously close the island of Salamis is to the mainland. Xerxes must have believed he would have no trouble crossing the narrow stretch of sea to slaughter the Athenian refugees.

Every male over seventeen joined the fleet. Some Athenians had argued in favour of defending the Acropolis. It was wrong, they thought, to abandon the holy places to the enemy. They sought the advice of Athena, the city's protecting goddess. The priestess said that Athena's sacred snake had not come out to eat its piece of honey cake. This meant that Athena herself had left the Acropolis and gone to Salamis to fight with the fleet. In spite of this, a handful of soldiers decided to stay and do what they could to save the holy places. Apollo's oracle had mentioned a 'wooden wall', which most people took to mean the Athenian fleet, but the soldiers built a real wooden wall as a safeguard.

When the Persian army reached Athens, the city was deserted except for the defenders of

the Acropolis. The Persians occupied the AREOPAGUS, a hill where, according to myth, the war god Ares had once been tried by his fellow immortals for the murder of Halirrhothius, son of Poseidon. Ares had been acquitted because there had been no witnesses. The Persians shot flaming arrows at the wooden wall, setting it on fire, and eventually broke into the citadel, smashing or burning the fortifications, temples, monuments and statues.

THE BATTLE OF SALAMIS

Determined to follow up his 'victory' in Athens, Xerxes was impatient to destroy the allied fleet. He was confident that the allies would eventually start squabbling among themselves. He called a council of his naval officers who agreed that the attack should take place as soon as possible. The one dissenting voice came from the only woman on the council, Queen Artemisia of Halicarnassus, but she was overruled. Xerxes joined battle with the Athenians off the coast of Salamis.

Nobody knows exactly what happened at the battle of Salamis. One fact, though, is clear. Xerxes had too many ships. They were lured into a narrow channel by the Athenians and their allies and were unable to manoeuvre. The Athenian squadron rammed into the high-decked Phoenician galleys and smashed their oars or knocked gaping holes in their sides.

Xerxes, sitting under his golden canopy,

Persian soldiers breach the wooden stockade, built by the Athenians after consulting Apollo's oracle, and lay waste to the ancient Acropolis.

must have felt more and more foolish as his fleet began to crumble. When he saw Queen Artemisia capture an allied ship, he commented that his women were fighting like men and his men like women. Some of his Phoenician captains had fought bravely but their ships had been wrecked on the shore. They reported to Xerxes and asked for further instructions. Enraged by their inability to defeat the Athenians, he had them all beheaded.

When it became obvious that the Persian fleet was beaten, Xerxes ordered that a bridge of boats be built from the mainland to Salamis so that he could get at the Athenians and kill them himself. An attempt was made, but so

In the naval battle of Salamis, the Persians tried to block the passage of Athenian ships. But the Athenians rammed the Persian vessels and destroyed half their fleet.

late in the year, the sea was far too rough.

All Xerxes could do was to go home. Still claiming a famous victory, he left his general, Mardonius, in charge of a large army in the north and returned to Sardis. There he organized a magnificent victory parade. The only disappointment was that the gold chariot with the statue of Mazda, chief of the Persian gods, had been lost during the campaign.

At Delphi the allies erected a colossal statue of Apollo holding the prow of a Persian warship. They also sacrificed captured ships to Poseidon, Athena and the hero god Ajax, who was worshipped at Salamis.

In the following year, a large army commanded by Pausanias, nephew of Leonidas, won a decisive victory over the remains of the Persian army at Plataea. The one Spartan who had been disgraced for not dying with his comrades at Thermopylae retrieved his reputation at Plataea. Mardonius was killed during the battle. The Spartan king, Leotychidas, commanding the allied navy, crushed the Persian fleet at the battle of Mycale. With their defeats, control of the Aegean passed out of the hands of the 'Great King'. Although the threat of another Persian invasion did not disappear, it now seemed unlikely.

CHAPTER 5

Religion

Religion in these ancient times was a very important and very personal matter but it was not well organized. There were many gods, but nothing was written down about them to tell people who the gods were or what powers they possessed. People did not study their religion or gather together regularly to pray at places of worship. In fact,

The unfinished Doric temple at Segesta, in Sicily, dating from the fifth century B.C.

people's ideas about their gods varied from town to town. The Apollo who lived at Delphi might seem very different from the Apollo who was born at Delos. And a stranger visiting Olympia might have looked at the statue of Apollo on the eastern pediment of the Temple of Zeus and wondered which of the gods it was supposed to represent.

GODS AND HEROES

In prehistoric times, as tribes jostled and shoved one another down the mainland and onto the islands of the Aegean, they brought their gods and goddesses with them. Some seem to have come from the Middle East, others from as far away as India. By the time of Pericles, the stories about the lives of the gods and their families had become so tangled and contradictory that it was difficult for ordinary people to say who all these superhuman beings were or why they behaved as they did.

The main advantage a god had over a human being was that he never appeared to grow old. He might in fact be so old that he had forgotten who his father or his wife was, or how many children he had. Yet he would still look eighteen, or forty, or fifty, or whatever age best suited his image.

There were three main branches of the rambling divine family. The ruling branch consisted of the OLYMPIANS, and the family home was Mount Olympus, though individual members had temples of their own all over the known world.

Although everybody knew that there were twelve Olympians, nobody could be sure exactly who they were. There was no problem with Zeus, Hera, Poseidon, Apollo, Artemis, Hermes, Hestia and Ares. The others were more doubtful. Some people claimed that Demeter and Dionysus were Olympians, some denied it.

Then came the lesser gods and goddesses. They were probably older than the Olympians and were more closely connected to the earth and even the region beneath. Hades was god of the underworld. Some people said that he was the brother of Zeus and Poseidon, but he does not ever appear to have been accepted as an Olympian. There were river gods, sea gods, gods of mountains and groves, winds and breezes, the sun and the moon, protectors of the fields and flocks, like Pan and Silenus, and dozens of local gods who seemed more approachable than the lofty Olympians.

The third group were the great heroes of mythology who had become demi-gods. Sometimes they were the offspring of a human and an immortal. The father of Achilles was a mortal, his mother a sea goddess. Poor Theseus, an early king of Athens, could never be sure who his father was. His mother had spent a night in bed with both Aegeus, who was too drunk to remember what happened, and the god Poseidon. Herakles was one of the many sons of Zeus born from an adulterous affair with a human.

These and other heroes, being part human, eventually died. Many cities could point to their tombs. It was believed that after their deaths, the heroes joined the other gods and looked after the interests of the cities that had been dear to them. The people of Salamis once dug up some giant bones. They decided that they had belonged to the hero Ajax, who fought at Troy. Ajax soon became a sort of patron saint of Salamis.

PRIESTS AND SEERS

Nowadays priests are thought of as people dedicated to leading their communities in worship, meditation and religious rites. But there was no idea, in Athens or elsewhere, of a priest having a special calling. He was not expected to be 'more holy' or to lead a 'better life' than others. In fact, he was an ordinary citizen who assisted in family or public acts of sacrifice, saw that the temple buildings, shrines and altars were properly cared for, and made sure that the gifts and money intended for the gods or deposited in the temple for safekeeping were not stolen. In some places the right to be a priest was granted to a particular family. Some priests inherited the post from their fathers.

Public religion – the organization of festivals, games and temple rituals – was originally in the hands of the kings or aristocrats who ruled the city. The word 'aristocracy' means literally 'government by the best', usually a small, privileged class. In Athens and other places where there was a democracy, the organization and

A white bull is led to the altar to be sacrificed to the gods.

arrangement of religious events passed into the hands of the elected city officials.

In the home, the father of the family was responsible for religion. Every house, indeed every part of the house, had its own protecting deities. There was always a shrine to Hestia, goddess of home life, and another to Zeus, who protected the building.

The first temples were probably made of wood or mud bricks. No example has survived.

Later temples were built of stone and marble. Inside there was only a magnificent statue of the god and a treasury where gifts were kept. Citizens might go into the temple and pray in front of the statue. They would then leave a gift for the god. Victors in the games might hand over their prizes. After the battle of Marathon, Miltiades offered his helmet to Zeus in the temple at Olympia.

The conduct of the gods may not have been very different from that of ordinary people. To us their behaviour often seems outrageous. Their advantage over mortals was that they were wiser, more cunning and more powerful. If you wanted to win a battle, it was a good idea to have Ares on your side. If you wanted to build a temple, Apollo knew how to do it.

There were certain crimes that offended the gods. These included mistreating a guest or abusing the hospitality of a host, breaking an oath, murdering a member of your family and leaving a body unburied. But perhaps the worst were impiety, pride and blasphemy. The gods would punish such crimes very severely. They could destroy people or nations who offended them in a number of ways. Plague – a speciality of Apollo –

The bronze helmet dedicated by Miltiades, after the victory of Marathon, to Zeus at Olympia.

earthquakes, thunderbolts, famine, flood and shipwreck were just a few. Sometimes it was possible to anger a god without knowing it. If a city was struck down by the plague, the chances were that somebody had done something to upset a god. The offender would then consult a seer in order to find out what was wrong.

A seer had many ways of discovering the will of the gods. Apollo's priestess at Delphi chewed laurel leaves and waited for inspiration. The entrails of a sacrificed animal could be studied. The feeding habits of sacred snakes could provide clues. A seer might watch a flight of birds and say to himself, 'If they swoop to the left, Ares wants us to fight. If they swoop to the right, we should run away.' He might enter a grove sacred to one of the gods and listen to the murmur of the wind in the trees or the rustle of fallen leaves. If the god's message was unclear and confusing, it was up to the seer to interpret it.

ALTARS AND SACRIFICE

Sacrifice was an important part of life. If a man had been successful, if his farm, for example, had produced plenty of crops and animals, if his side had won a battle, if the ships he had sent to trade had come home safely, or if his wife had given birth to a boy, then that good fortune was due to the gods. If you kept on offering the gods gifts and sharing your food and drink with them, they would approve of you and look after you.

The central object in any act of worship was the altar. There were altars everywhere: in front of temples, in the theatre, in the home, in woodland groves, in the fields, at the boundaries of the town and in public places. On the altar burned a fire. Here the priest would burn incense and part of the offerings that citizens brought for sacrifice. The smoke and aroma would please the god. The animal victim to be sacrificed had its throat cut in a special way. The ritual varied from place to place and from god to god. Then the flesh was cut up. Some of it, usually the thigh bones and the fat, was burned on the altar for the gods. The rest was barbecued on spits and eaten by the human participants in the ritual. Other things, too, could be sacrificed. At the start of a drinking party, wine was poured on the earth as a LIBATION, or gift, to the gods. Oil, cakes, locks of hair or even a ship or two were acceptable.

An older form of sacrifice existed in some places and seemed to be associated with a more ancient race of gods. An animal would be held down, its throat cut and the blood allowed to soak into the earth. Then the victim's body was burned on the altar.

Most citizens of the fifth century B.C. regarded human sacrifice with terror. They believed it had happened in prehistoric times, and many famous myths are concerned with it. By the time of Pericles it probably did not exist. But a story that the later historian Plutarch tells of Themistocles before the battle of Salamis refers to one such event:

Themistocles was sacrificing near the admiral's flagship. Three handsome prisoners were brought to him, dressed in rich clothes and wearing gold ornaments. They were said to be the sons of Sandauce, Xerxes' sister. As soon as Euphranites, the seer, caught sight of them, a pillar of fire shot up from the altar, and a sneeze was heard from the right hand side, which is a good omen. At this, Euphranites grabbed Themistocles by the right hand and ordered him to cut off the young men's forelocks, to offer prayers and to sacrifice them to the god Dionysus, 'Eater of Flesh', and, if this was done, the fleet would have a great victory.

Plutarch goes on to say that the crowd then forced Themistocles to carry out the slaughter, but adds that the story was told to him. In all probability, it was fiction.

THE AFTERLIFE

The dead heroes of Homer's epic poems travelled to an underworld where they lived as 'shades', wishing they were back on earth. Many people did believe in an afterlife for some. The mysteries celebrated at Eleusis in honour of Demeter and her daughter Persephone probably included the promise of a happy afterlife for those pilgrims who, after long ceremonies of purification, were initiated into the secrets of the cult. Worshippers of Dionysus included women. Some of the god's secret rites involved drunken and frenzied dancing during which, so some people believed, animals and even children were ritually slaughtered. Somehow the worship of Dionysus, a god who was himself once torn to bits, eaten by humans and brought back to life, became confused with stories of Orpheus, a musician and singer who was also hacked to pieces by his female followers. We are not sure how, but it seems that abandonment to Dionysus could result in eternal life.

APOLLO

Apollo was one of the most popular gods. Stories about him give a good idea of how people thought of the supernatural beings who controlled their destinies and rewarded or punished their good and wicked deeds.

Zeus had a love affair with the nymph Leto. He turned himself and Leto into quails so that his wife, Hera, would not find out about it. But Hera discovered the truth and sent a serpent, Python, to chase Leto all over the world. She also forbade the nymph to give birth to the twins she was carrying in any place where the sun shone. On the floating island of Delos, Artemis was born first. Then she helped her mother give birth to Apollo. It took nine days. He was born in a sacred grove between an olive tree and a date palm. At four days old, he was fully grown. He commanded that Delos be fixed in its place in the Aegean and that nobody should give birth or die there. Then the young god took a bow and arrow, went to Mount Parnassus, where Python lived, and began to shoot at it. The poor serpent, which had only been obeying Hera's orders, fled to Delphi, and begged for protection from MOTHER EARTH. But Apollo chased Python into the sacred shrine and finished it off.

Apollo depicted in his temple at Delphi before the sacred stone that was the 'omphalos', or navel, alleged to be the centre of the earth.

Apollo kills Python, the legendary snake of Mount Parnassus, in his shrine at Delphi. To commemorate the event, Apollo founded the Pythian Games.

Mother Earth was furious and complained to Apollo's father. Zeus ordered his son to undergo ritual purification, but Apollo decided to take a holiday first, for he had another score to settle on behalf of his mother. A woman named Niobe, who had fourteen beautiful children, had laughed at Leto because she had only two. Apollo and Artemis now took their bows and arrows and killed all Niobe's children. Niobe wept so much that she turned into a river.

Zeus never gained the respect of his son. Apollo became so irritated by his father that he, Hera, Poseidon and the other members of the family seized Zeus while he was having a nap and tied him up. The more the father of the gods ranted and raved, the louder Apollo laughed. There was an argument as to who should be chief god in place of Zeus. But the nymph Thetis, seeing that the row might destroy the family, set Zeus free. Apollo and Poseidon, as ringleaders of the revolt, were punished by having to build the city of Troy.

Apollo never married but had a number of children by nymphs and mortals. One son, Asclepius, became a brilliant doctor, and could even bring dead people back to life. This upset Hades, who feared he might be out of a job if the dead were raised. He complained to Zeus, who shot a thunderbolt at Asclepius and burned him up. Apollo was furious. Zeus had some gigantic, one-eyed servants called cyclopes, who made weapons and armour for him. Apollo killed them in revenge. For this crime Zeus sentenced his son to a year's hard labour as a shepherd.

Originally, Apollo had been god of crops and cattle, but his sacred herd was kidnapped by his half-brother, Hermes. Apollo was very angry at first. Then he discovered that Hermes had invented the very first musical instrument, the lyre, from a tortoiseshell and the gut of one of his own cows. Apollo decided he wanted to be god of music. He exchanged his herds for Hermes' lyre. Hermes also gave Apollo a set of reed pipes. Apollo offered these to the old nature god, Pan, forcing him in return to teach him the secrets of prophecy. He then moved to Delphi and seized control of the oracle.

Apollo had many loves, although one or two girls did turn him down. The nymph Daphne was the priestess of Mother Earth. She ran from the god and he chased her. But Mother Earth turned her into a laurel bush. Apollo made a wreath of its leaves to remind him of Daphne.

Hyacinthus was a Spartan prince. Apollo spent so much time with him that Hyacinthus forgot all his other friends, including Zephyrus, the West Wind. One day Apollo was teaching Hyacinthus to throw the discus. Zephyrus, jealous at not being allowed to join in, caught the metal disc and threw it back at the boy's head, killing him instantly. All Apollo could do was turn Hyacinthus's blood into the flowers we know today by the same name and write his signature on the leaves.

Apollo was the god of many things including the sun, prophecy, healing, archery, music, truth and common sense. It was, however, his oracle at Delphi that made him such a powerful influence on every aspect of private and public life.

CHAPTER 6

The Theatre

The origins of drama – compositions for performance on a stage – are lost in the remoteness of time. Throughout the world religion and theatre have always been closely linked. The plays that were performed in Athens at the time of Pericles were always part of a religious festival. But we do not know where tragedy and comedy really originated, and a lot of conflicting information has been written on the subject.

The figure of the playwright, Menander, sits here holding the mask of one of the characters in his plays, with masks for two other characters on the table.

SONG AND DANCE

The city-states were mostly simple farming communities. Religious rituals and festivals played an important part in their lives. There were ceremonies and sacrifices to ensure the protection of the gods when the seed was sown, when the animals were mated, when the grapes and olives were being tended and when their juice was turned into wine and oil. Harvest was a time to rejoice and thank the gods for their gifts. One form of worship was the ritual dance.

Wine, too, was of great importance at these celebrations. And Dionysus, god of the vintage, was also the god who presided over the major Athenian drama festivals.

Dance was often accompanied by song. Choral singing was as popular in the sixth and fifth centuries B.C. in the city-states as it once was in the valleys of Wales. There were fifty members in a choir, which was all-male, consisting of boys, youths or men. They sang hymns in honour of a god, usually in competitions and at religious festivals. The hymns were very long and related the deeds and life story of the god or goddess being praised. Songs that won the prize were added to the choir's future programme. The performers were accompanied by wind instruments, stringed instruments and percussion. Although some of the words are known, none of the music has survived.

EPIC POETRY

The people of the city-states were not great writers and readers. They were mainly thinkers,

31

talkers and listeners, who wrote things down only if they needed to keep a record. Epic poetry, however, was intended to be performed before an audience. Not only did it entertain, it contained great lessons for life. The stories of gods and heroes taught people how to behave. Homer's epic stories of the gods' involvement in the Trojan war and the wanderings of Odysseus were sung in public. It is probable that they had been handed down from generation to generation for hundreds of years before they were actually written down. Some of the stories of the poet Hesiod, too, can be traced back to the Hittite empire, Babylon and Sumeria.

The drama that developed in fifth-century Athens became a popular form of religious celebration. Most of the plots of the tragedies were taken from the epics. While the events were often based on mythology, the characters in the plays thought and behaved like the people in the audience. The comedies were different. Although gods and heroes often appeared, most of these plays dealt with issues of the time.

ACTORS AND THEATRES

In the days before democracy, Athens was ruled by tyrants, kings who sometimes took power illegally and by force. Legend has it that the first actor was Thespis, who arrived at the time of the tyrant Pisistratus (540-527 B.C.). Thespis travelled in a cart that doubled as a platform from which he could speak his part or as a backdrop in front of which he could perform. He was accompanied by a chorus of fifty male singers and dancers. And he brought about another great change. Previously the chorus all sang together, but Thespis separated himself from the chorus. Instead of everyone saying the same thing, it now became possible to hold a dialogue or tell a story. Probably the nearest thing we have to Thespian drama today is the oratorio – Handel's *Messiah* or Bach's *Christmas Oratorio*, for example – in which the soloists and the chorus sing in turn.

By the end of the fifth century B.C., drama was being taken by touring actors and choruses to other cities. And by this time performances were given in real theatres. The theatre of Dionysus in Athens is built in a natural amphitheatre on the hill below the Acropolis. Originally the seats were made of wood. The performing area – called the ORCHESTRA – was a circle, very much like a circus ring. Behind the circle, facing the audience, was a primitive *skene* (scene-building). It was a simple wooden structure, perhaps with a door through which the one and only actor could make his entrance. In front were a couple of steps on which he could stand. He would play as many parts as the play required, male or female, young or old, mortal or immortal. Sometimes, particularly if he was playing a god or goddess, he would stand on top of the scene-building. Obviously there was not much action. Most of the events described by the actor or the chorus took place offstage.

In due course, the wooden seats in the amphitheatre at Athens were replaced by stone ones. If you look at the remains of the

An actor holds in his hands a mask and a sword.

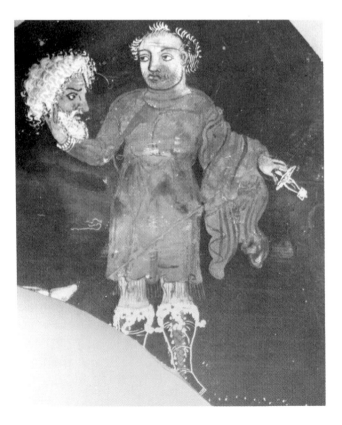

The well-preserved theatre at Segesta, Sicily, showing stone seats and part of the performing area.

theatre today, you will get little idea of what it was like at the time of Pericles. Later on, the Romans made 'improvements'. They reduced the circle to a semi-circle and put up a massive stone scene-building. Circular stone theatres were also built at Delphi and Epidaurus. The one at Epidaurus is the best preserved. It has the full circle as the performing area and is still in use.

THE DRAMATISTS

We know the names of about 150 dramatists who wrote tragedies in Athens during the fifth century B.C. We have examples of the work of only three of them: Aeschylus, Sophocles and Euripides. But we are still finding scraps of plays today, especially in ancient Egyptian rubbish dumps.

Aeschylus (525-456 B.C.), who fought at Marathon, had the revolutionary idea of using two actors instead of just one. It was now possible to write a play with a conversation in it or even a quarrel. Plays were written in groups of four and performed during the course of one day. There were three linking tragedies – rather like a modern serial or the acts of a full-length play. These were followed by a satyr play, a sort of song and dance farce which may have treated the themes of the tragedy in a comical manner. The only three-play cycle that has survived is by Aeschylus, although the satyr play is missing. This is the cycle known as the *Oresteia*. It tells the story of King Agamemnon who, after returning from Troy, is murdered by his wife Clytemnestra and her lover Aegisthus. Agamemnon's son, Orestes, urged on by his sister, Elektra, avenges his father's death by killing them both. He, in turn, is punished by being pursued by the goddesses of revenge known as the FURIES. Eventually Apollo and Athena untangle the problems and order is restored.

Sophocles (496-406 B.C.) added a third actor to his tragedies. It is said that as a boy Sophocles was chosen to be the 'leader of Athenian youth' at the Salamis victory celebrations. Later he became one of Pericles' co-generals. He was considered one of the

greatest tragedians of the age. His most famous surviving plays concern the legendary Theban king, Oedipus ('swollen feet'), who killed his father by mistake, married his mother in ignorance and tore his eyes out when he discovered what he had done.

Euripides (485-406 B.C.) wrote about ninety-two tragedies. We have seventeen of them. He also wrote the only satyr play that has survived, The Cyclops. Euripides reduced the role of the chorus to a series of musical interludes. The Athenians thought him original, daring and modern, and his support came mainly from an enthusiastic younger generation. The Bacchae, perhaps his most famous play, is about the revenge taken by the god Dionysus

upon Pentheus, a king who refused to allow his people to worship him. Pentheus is set upon and killed by a band of female devotees, including his own mother. Under the god's intoxicating influence, she has mistaken her handsome son for a lion. Two of Euripides' greatest tragedies deal with families torn apart by powerful women. In *Hippolytus* a young

The procession into the theatre of Dionysus at Athens, headed by musicians and men leading black panthers, followed by the white bull, adorned with flowers and ribbons, that is to be sacrificed to the god.

prince refuses to respond to the advances made by his stepmother, who plots his destruction. It is the first play we know of in which a death occurs on stage. Violent events were usually reported by messengers. *Medea* is a play about a woman who, abandoned by Theseus, legendary king of Athens, murders her children by him. Euripides is the first creator of great women's roles, although the parts would have been played by men.

PERICLES PRODUCES A PLAY

In 472 B.C. Pericles was chosen to produce a play for the spring Dionysia, or drama festival. It was a great honour for the twenty-two-year-old Athenian, suggesting that a group of influential families were grooming the boy for a political career. It probably also meant that his father, Xanthippus, had died and that Pericles had inherited his estate and money. He would not otherwise have been able to afford the heavy costs involved as a CHOREGUS (producer).

In ancient Athens, the Great, or City, Dionysia was the most important of the four annual festivals in honour of Dionysus. It was both a religious occasion and a competition. For many months before the festival, playwrights who wished to take part would submit their work to the ARCHON, the city's highest elected official. Each work consisted of three tragedies and a comic satyr play. The archon and his committee would choose the three best sets of plays for the competition. One of the works selected in 472 B.C. was by Aeschylus; and one of the plays performed on that occasion, *The Persians*, still survives.

Aeschylus's play was unusual in that it dealt with a contemporary theme, showing what happened when news of the defeat at Salamis was brought to the Persian court. Plays that treated modern subjects were not unknown but were considered to be risky. A few years earlier, the archon had chosen a play by Phrynichus called *The Taking of Miletus*. It described the suffering of the town of Miletus under the Persians. Athens had abandoned Miletus to its fate after withdrawing from the Ionian revolt. The 17,000 people in the audience had burst into tears and were so over-

Head of Sophocles, the celebrated Athenian tragic playwright.

come with grief that it took them days to recover. The city fined Phrynichus and banned all future productions of his play. However, the tragedy probably strengthened the Athenian resolve to resist the Persian onslaught it was about to face.

The city allocated actors to each of the successful dramatists. It paid the actors, provided their costumes and masks, covered their expenses and supplied the props. It also appointed a choregus for each of the three cycles. This producer had to pay for the training, costumes, music and expenses of the members of the chorus. The producer nominated for the plays of Aeschylus was Pericles.

There followed many frantic weeks of rehearsal and preparation. Masks were made, boots and costumes stitched. Because the theatre was so vast, a very elaborate and formal style of acting, speaking and singing was used. Thanks to the design of the theatre, it was possible to hear clearly, even from the back row. Seeing presented more of a problem, but this did not matter too much because the masks worn by the actors showed one fixed expression. The platform soles of the boots gave the actors extra height and made them look more impressive. There was very little scenery, but props, such as weapons, torches and even chariots, had to be procured. Dancers had to learn their complex steps. The musicians had to be taught to work with the chorus.

THE FESTIVAL

The first day of the festival began with elaborate and colourful processions led by boys in their second year of military training. There was music and singing. The white bull that was to be sacrificed to Dionysus, decorated with flowers and ribbons, was near the front of the procession. The boys took the statue of Dionysus from its shrine at the ACADEMIA the sacred grove just outside the city wall. It was dressed in new clothes and garlands and carried to the theatre, followed by the god's various emblems and symbols. Then came the chief archon, the other archons, the five citizens selected by lot to judge the competition, the producers, authors, actors, choruses and everyone else. At the altar in the centre of the orchestra, the bull was sacrificed. The boys then set up the statue of the god.

The important citizens and their guests, who probably included visitors from other cities, sat at the front. All adult male Athenians, but no women, were obliged to attend. Those who could not afford the entrance charge of two OBOLS were paid for out of public funds.

The rest of the day was taken up with choral singing. Ten choirs, five of men and five of boys, competed for the prizes, which were awarded at the end of the day. The night was spent in feasting and drinking.

On the second day, between three and five comedies, also selected by the archon and his committee, were performed. The second night was spent in more drinking. We are told that many young men became so completely drunk that they slept where they fell.

There then followed three days when each of the chosen writers presented his complete cycle of plays. It must have been difficult for many of the audience sitting in the bright morning sunlight, feeling hot and hung-over from the night before, to concentrate on Aeschylus's powerful dramas.

Before the plays began, and presumably after the daily sacrifices, the city herald would present those nineteen-year-olds whose fathers had been killed in battle. These orphans would have been brought up and received their military training at the city's expense. Now, dressed in their brand new armour, they were welcomed by the citizens. The herald announced, 'The city dismisses them with many prayers for their good fortune, each to his own home. Show them to seats of honour in this theatre'.

In 472 B.C. the cycle by Aeschylus, produced by Pericles, won the prize. *The Persians* contains a description of the battle of Salamis fought only ten years earlier. It must have made a big impression on those many members of the audience who had taken part in the battle or at least watched it from the shore.

Aeschylus's prize was a crown of ivy, presented by the chief archon. Pericles won the right to set up a memorial to his success as a producer. The best actor had his name inscribed on the city's role of honour. Such rewards might appear rather small after all the expense and effort involved, but the Athenians considered fame and honour more important than financial rewards.

Aeschylus, it would seem, was not a good loser. At a later festival, when the prize was awarded to Sophocles instead of himself, he left Athens and went to live in Sicily. Here the great playwright met his death. He had written more than eighty plays, transforming dramatic art and elevating the language. He was a deeply patriotic and religious man. His simple but beautiful epitaph speaks of him not as a great writer but as a man who fought against tyrants for the independence of his city:

Beneath this stone, Euphorion's son,
   Aeschylus the Athenian
Who died by the fields of Gela, golden with
   ripe wheat.
The Field of Marathon still sings of his valour
            — the strength of his arm
As could the longhaired Persian
            — who felt it.

CHAPTER 7

The Olympic Games

On the plain of Olympia was a sacred precinct called the grove of Altis. In ancient times it contained an oracle of Mother Earth. Hera, the wife of Zeus, was later worshipped there. Then Zeus himself took over. Visitors to the grove hung their offerings to the god in its trees.

It is said that the Olympic games were started by the hero god Herakles. One of twelve labours that he was challenged to perform was to clean out the stables of Augeas, king of Elis, which contained 3,000 oxen. Herakles completed the task in a single day and celebrated by founding the games.

A more likely explanation is that these were originally funeral games held in honour of a local dead hero. To the ancients, it would not have seemed inappropriate to celebrate a funeral with a day of sport. The most famous funeral games were those held by Achilles for his friend Patroclus, described in the *Iliad*.

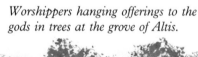

Worshippers hanging offerings to the gods in trees at the grove of Altis.

THE CHARIOT OF PELOPS

A third version of the Olympic story concerns Pelops, the son of Tantalus. One day Tantalus invited Zeus and the other Olympians to dinner, and served up his son to them. The gods, recognizing what was on their plates, were shocked and horrified. All except Demeter, who had her mind on other things, her daughter Persephone having been kidnapped. She took a mouthful of the stew before she realized what she was doing. Zeus sent Tantalus down to the underworld and ordered Hades to collect the parts of Pelops' body and put them back together again. The only missing piece was the shoulder that Demeter had eaten, so a special ivory one was made to replace it. It must have been the world's first artificial limb.

When Pelops stepped out of the cauldron alive and well, Poseidon gave him a job as his cupbearer. In addition to being god of the sea, Poseidon was god of horses. Being surrounded all day by horses and chariots, Pelops soon became an expert rider. He fell in love with a girl from Pisa, near Olympia, named Hippodameia, whose father, Oenomaus, owned splendid racing stables. Hippodameia was only permitted to marry the young man who could beat her father in a chariot race. All losers had their heads cut off, finding a place in a temple of skulls that Oenomaus planned to build.

Pelops asked Poseidon for his help. The

The gods and goddesses of Olympia watch Pelops rising from the cauldron, restored to life.

god readily gave his friend a gold chariot and a team of winged horses. The chariot could travel over land or sea without getting its wheels wet. Pelops tested it out by taking his friend Gillius across the Aegean Sea. Pelops drove so fast that Gillius died of shock.

On the day of the race, Pelops persuaded a mechanic to fit his opponent's chariot with an axle made of wax. The chariot crashed and Oenomaus was killed. Pelops and Hippodameia lived happily ever after. Pelops introduced horse-racing into the Olympic games. The ghost of Oenomaus is said to have haunted an altar at one end of the hippodrome, or race course, and frightened passing horses.

When he died, Pelops' tomb and shrine were built in the sacred grove at Olympia. Some people said that the Olympic games must have begun as funeral celebrations for the dead hero. As for Pelops' ivory shoulder, it was sent separately to Pisa where it was kept in its own shrine.

It is thought that the first games, to which all were invited, took place in 776 B.C. They were held every fourth year for a thousand years. Games were celebrated at Delphi in honour of Apollo, at Corinth in honour of Poseidon and at Nemea in honour of Zeus. But the games held at Olympia, also dedicated to Zeus, were by far the most famous and prestigious. To get to Olympia, the contestants travelled by sea and then up the River Alpheios. As many of the city-states were often at war with one another, a truce was declared for the period of the festival. The truce was ordered by Zeus himself, so it was not often broken. Three heralds carrying staffs of office and wearing crowns of olive leaves journeyed from Elis, the state where Olympia was situated, to every other city-state. They proclaimed the universal truce and invited everybody – except, of course, women and slaves – to the Olympic games.

The site of Olympia has been under excavation by German archaeologists and many others since 1936. They have found some interesting remains, including temples, altars and tombs.

Oenomaus's chariot crashes in the fatal race against Pelops, his daughter's suitor.

According to Pausanias, a visitor to Olympia in A.D. 140, the mound of ash on the Altar of Zeus rose high above the altar surface.

THE SACRED PRECINCTS

The Altar of Zeus was believed to have been the holiest place in the sacred precincts 500 years before the time of Pericles. Legend said that it was built on the spot where Zeus had hurled a thunderbolt from Mount Olympus in order to establish his claim to the hallowed grove. The ashes from the sacrifice were never removed from the altar. Instead they were mixed into a paste with water from the sacred river. Pausanias, a visitor to Olympia in A.D. 140, reported that the mound of ash rose some metres off the altar.

The Temple of Zeus, probably the most famous temple of its time, contained the statue of Zeus, one of the seven wonders of the ancient world. The temple was finished in 456 B.C. The huge statue was designed by Phidias, creator of the statue of Athena in the Parthenon. Pausanias described it:

> The god sits on a throne. He is made of ivory and gold and he wears a wreath like a spray of olive leaves. In his right hand is a gold and ivory [statue of] Victory, in his left a sceptre on which is perched his eagle. His sandals are gold. His robe is gold and

decorated with animals and lilies. The throne is inlaid with gold, ivory, ebony and precious stones.

The statue of Zeus remained in his temple for nearly 900 years. Later it was stolen and eventually destroyed by fire.

The Temple of Hera was the oldest in the sacred grove. It is said that, before the people of Elis were converted to the worship of Zeus, they chiefly honoured Hera, his wife. Husband and wife both had statues in her temple, and inside there was also a gold and ivory table on which prizes for the games, olive-leaf victory crowns, were placed.

The site of the sacred olive tree, perhaps the oldest in the grove, has been found. In very early times it had been given a protective fence. At the festival a boy cut branches from the tree with a golden sickle.

The Pelopion, or grave of Pelops, has been excavated. A number of other people had

Excavated temple columns from Olympia.

been buried there, dating back almost 2,000 years before Pericles' time.

The Prytaneion, built in about 470 B.C., housed the sacred hearth of the goddess Hestia. The fire on this altar was never allowed to go out, and from it were lit the flames of other altars in the sanctuary.

Many other temples, shrines, altars, treasuries and administrative buildings stood in the precinct. There were also statues to the gods. The victor of each game was allowed to put up a statue of himself. Few have been found, apart from the bases on which they were placed.

TRACES OF THE GAMES

There are impressive remains of race courses at Olympia, but most of these did not exist at the time of Pericles. During this period all running tracks were straight, not curved like modern ones, and the finishing line for races was near the Altar of Zeus. Spectators sat on the nearby Hill of Cronos. Later a magnificent stadium was constructed outside the sacred grove.

No trace has been found of the hippodrome at Olympia. This is because the River Alpheios changed direction a few hundred years ago and flooded the area where the hippodrome had once stood. The hippodrome must have been over 150 metres wide and more than half a kilometre long. It was used both for horse races and chariot races. Ancient writers say that the two turning points were marked by statues of Pelops and Hippodameia.

There had been baths at Olympia since the fifth century B.C. Unusually, there were hot water baths and steam baths. Some people, probably Spartans, complained that the hot water turned men soft. They were in constant use, however, until the first century B.C. when a more elaborate building was put up by the Romans, who were expert domestic engineers.

The only swimming pool we know of was at Olympia. It measured about 25 metres by 15 metres. It was used for the enjoyment of the athletes and not for competitions.

THE EVENTS

As the years passed, more and more events were added to the Olympic games. At the time of Pericles these would have included various races and other contests of skill, strength and stamina.

The three standard types of foot race were a sprint, a middle-distance and a long-distance. There was also a race run wearing armour and carrying a shield. There was, of course, no marathon until modern times.

The five events of the pentathlon were javelin, discus, long jump, running and wrestling. Apart from running, wrestling was the only one that was also a separate event. A pentathlon for boys was introduced in 628 B.C., but it was discontinued after its first year. The Spartans claimed it was because a Spartan boy won it.

Boxing was the bloodiest and most popular sport. Boxers wore no gloves but bound their hands with leather thongs.

The *penkration* was a combination of boxing and wrestling. Most things were legal except kicking, biting and trying to poke out the opponent's eyes.

Chariot races were enormously popular. A team consisted of four horses. A two-horse race was added in 408 B.C.

Horse-racing was a bareback event both for horses and riders. It must have been very uncomfortable. A race for mares was discontinued in 444 B.C.

The *apene* was a mule-cart race, which must have seemed very tame after the thrills and spills of the four-horse chariot race. The only people who were interested in it, or who were any good at it, were Sicilian colonists, and it, too, was eventually discontinued.

Competitors in all the events were naked. Two amusing stories explain why this was the rule. According to the first, in the days when shorts were worn, one competitor in a foot race started to lose them, pulled them off and went on to win. This set a trend. The other version is that a popular competitor, who was about to win a race, lost his shorts, which

A distance foot race in the Olympic games. Competitors ran naked and winners received crowns of olive branches.

tripped him up. The judges decided to make sure it could never happen again. By the time of Pericles, one of the jokes Athenians told about 'barbarians' was that they performed athletics with their clothes on.

Except for the priestesses of Demeter, women were not allowed near the Olympic games. In fact, there was a law which said that any woman found trying to watch any part of the festival would be thrown off a mountain. One woman was caught. She had disguised herself as a horse trainer in order to watch her son compete in the horse race. The boy won his event. His excited mother jumped over the barrier of the trainers' enclosure to congratulate him, but in doing so, it became clear she was not a man. She was granted a pardon, but the judges ruled that in future all trainers would also have to be naked.

Eventually women were permitted to hold their own games at Olympia every four years. They were held in honour of the goddess Hera. The only events were foot races.

THE FESTIVAL

Originally the games had lasted a single day. As the festival became more elaborate, it was extended to five days. The first event was the oath-taking. Judges and competitors stood in front of a statue of Zeus and swore not to cheat. Those caught cheating were fined or flogged in public. The judges carried sticks. During the boxing or wrestling matches, instead of shouting 'Break!', they beat the offender about the head and shoulders.

In the afternoon came boys' events. Then the rest of the day was spent in prayer and feasting.

The second day began with a procession of priests, judges and competitors to the hippodrome. After the usual sacrifice the equestrian events took place. The afternoon was for the pentathlon. In the evening the funeral rites of Pelops were celebrated. These included choral performances, victory parades and sacrifices in the sacred grove.

The third day opened with the great sacrifice. One hundred oxen were led in procession to the Altar of Zeus. Behind walked ambassadors from all the cities taking part in the games. At the altar the oxen were slaughtered and cut up. The priests burned the thigh bones and fat on the huge pile of ashes. The good meat was cooked for the evening's feast. The afternoon was devoted to the foot races.

The fourth day was set aside for boxing, wrestling and the race in armour.

On the fifth and last day there was a procession to the Temple of Zeus where the victors, wearing ribbons of wool round their heads, were crowned with olive wreaths. They were then showered with leaves and flowers and everybody trooped off for another feast.

CHAPTER 8

Pericles and Democracy

Pericles has been portrayed throughout history as a heroic champion of democracy, an incorruptible statesman, a great general and a much-loved Athenian. He is also remembered as the beautifier of the Acropolis in Athens. The truth, however, is that we know very little about Pericles. He was a very private man. Few of his contemporaries knew him well, and most of the information about him is based on the opinion of others. He left no letters or autobiographical writings. Three speeches he made to the people of Athens were later reported by the historian Thucydides, who explained that

A statue of Pericles. Most present-day information about the Athenian leader is coloured by the opinion of other writers.

what he had written contained the spirit of what Pericles said rather than the actual words.

Plutarch's life of Pericles came hundreds of years after the latter's death, although he did claim to have access to histories written in Pericles' own time, which have since been lost. Even though Plutarch appears to be praising Pericles as an honourable leader, between the lines, he seems to paint a picture of an arrogant man who brought his city to the brink of ruin and was only removed from office by his fellow citizens when it was too late to put matters right. We can see two

principal results of his government: first, the wonders of the Acropolis, paid for with plunder from his defenceless allies, and, second, the utter destruction of his own city-state and many others.

ATHENIAN DEMOCRACY

Until a very few years before the Persian wars began, Athens had been ruled by a family of tyrants. When they were expelled, a form of democracy was established. The highest authority in Athens was the Assembly, open to all citizens over eighteen, which met every two weeks and more often in times of crisis. The business of the Assembly was organized by a council of 500 citizens. Athens and its surrounding countryside were divided into ten units, called DEMES. These provided a list of their citizens who were over thirty years old, and from these lists fifty councillors were chosen by lot from each deme. A councillor served for one year only.

Athenians were often very late for Assembly meetings as they preferred to chat with their friends in the AGORA, or market-place. When the Assembly was due to begin the day's

Pericles addresses the Athenian Assembly on the Pnyx hill.

business, the city policemen walked rapidly across the square carrying a rope dripping with red paint. The only exit open was the one that led to the Pnyx, the hill on which the Assembly met. Anyone who did not move fast enough would get his clothes ruined.

Court cases were heard in front of massive juries of over 200 people. The crimes that were tried in the courts ranged from personal grievances and theft to disorderly conduct and immoral behaviour. There were no lawyers and everyone could speak for or against the accused. If the prisoner was not acquitted, he might be sentenced to a heavy fine, banishment or death by crucifixion. He might even be forced to commit suicide by taking poison.

GOVERNMENT OFFICIALS

The men who served on the council were called archons. The chief archon was called the *eponymos* archon because the year in which he served was named after him. The 'king' archon was in charge of religious affairs, another archon supervised the war office and the other six were responsible for justice.

These nine archons were chosen by lot from the group of 500 councillors selected by the demes. When they had completed their year's term of office, they became permanent members of the Areopagus, a sort of upper chamber where cases of murder were tried.

Some officers of the city-state were chosen by election. Each year Athens elected ten generals who had equal rights and served for a year. Pericles established a power base by getting himself elected general year after year after year. Architects, town planners and some priests were also elected.

Although we think of Athens as a real democracy, it would never have occurred to an Athenian man that there might be something not quite right about keeping slaves. Nor would he have dreamed of allowing a woman to go anywhere near the public government buildings, let alone have a vote. Only in Sparta were women expected to play any sort of responsible part in society.

CHAPTER 9

The Early Days of Pericles

The Athenian Assembly was steered and guided by factions – groups of citizens with common interests who banded together to push their points of view. A faction led by Ephialtes picked out Pericles as a promising young politician. When Ephialtes was murdered, Pericles inherited the leadership of the group. His enemies said Pericles himself was responsible for the murder, but they had no evidence.

Bronze wheels that were used by Athenian citizens to cast their votes. They were inserted into a special ballot box and counted later.

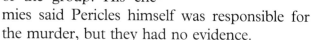

The poet Ion accused Pericles of being proud, disdainful and contemptuous of others. Friendlier colleagues said that he was simply reserved and dignified. They all agreed that he never laughed, never cracked jokes, never went to parties – except once, to a wedding, which he left before the drinking started – never in thirty years invited friends to dinner, and chose to speak in the Assembly only on matters of state importance. Other historians suggest that he was rather shy and had a big and rather odd-shaped head that made him self-conscious.

Thucydides, who knew Pericles, stated that his manner was aristocratic. He was able to rule Athens but, at the same time, appear to be only first among equals. He seems to have removed all his rivals, then made himself indispensable to the state. It got to the point where no decision could be made without Pericles' view first being heard.

PERICLES AND CIMON

An early rival of Pericles was Cimon, the son of Miltiades of Marathon fame. An aristocrat, who was well liked by the ordinary people, Cimon had fought the Persians, defeating their fleet in 466 B.C. and routing their land forces. Cimon turned his lands into public parks and provided free dinners for the poor. He believed that if Athens and Sparta could live together in peace, all the other city-states would be peaceful as well. There would also be less chance of further attacks by the Persians. He was supported by influential members of the Areopagus.

Pericles did not have enough money of his own to compete with Cimon in handouts to the people. He therefore devised the simple idea of spending large amounts of public money. Pericles got the Assembly to pay salaries to council members and jurors, and to spend lavishly on public works, bribes and festivals. There was never much thought about where the money was coming from.

Pericles regarded the Spartans as rivals and enemies. He would hardly have prospered in Sparta because the Spartans did not use money at all. To be caught with a wallet full of cash was punishable by death. Pericles looked on Cimon's efforts to establish friendly

The murder of the Athenian statesman, Ephialtes, whose death paved the way for the rise of Pericles.

relations between Sparta and Athens, the two strongest states on the western mainland, as almost treason. There was a system in Athens originally designed to prevent a would-be tyrant from rising to power. The citizen took a bit of broken pot, or *ostrakon*, and scratched upon it the name of anybody he did not like. When the pieces were counted, if more than 6,000 people had voted, the person with the most votes against him was 'ostracized', or banished, for ten years. Pericles got rid of Cimon by having him ostracized. His own lavish spending made him more popular.

Pericles had never been selected as an archon, so he was not a member of the Areopagus. He now persuaded the Assembly to take away nearly all the powers from the upper house. It was no longer concerned with important affairs of state and became merely a court for trying murderers and a place for old men to talk to one another.

The Spartans liked and trusted Cimon but were very suspicious of Pericles. During a border dispute, the Spartans sent an army and gave the Athenians a thrashing. Cimon unexpectedly returned to fight alongside his fellow citizens. Although Cimon wanted peace with Sparta, he was prepared to support his country 'right or wrong'. Pericles' friends, however, would not let him join in the battle in which many of Cimon's supporters died.

By now the Athenians realized they had made a big mistake and trusted Pericles too much. They recalled Cimon from exile, and he made peace with Sparta. Pericles had to tread more carefully until after Cimon's death in 450 B.C.

An ostrakon, *or pottery fragment, bearing the name of Cimon, the rival of Pericles, who was exiled by the Assembly.*

CHAPTER 10

The Delian League

Delos is an island in the centre of the Aegean Sea. It was a holy place of pilgrimage, for the god Apollo was thought to have been born there. The long, paved path to the god's sanctuary was guarded by a row of lions carved from white marble. Inside were shrines, statues of the Olympian gods, the temple itself and a massive statue of Apollo. The Persians had left Delos alone, not wishing to offend the god. After the war, in 478 B.C., the city-states met at Delos and formed an alliance against future invasions. All members of the Delian League made contributions according to their means. Athens provided most of the ships. Other states gave ships or money. The funds were placed under the protection of Apollo in the temple treasury on Delos.

ATHENS CONTROLS THE SEAS

Pericles, like Themistocles, knew that Athens was a natural sea-power. But because it was not an island, it needed a convenient port for control of the Aegean. Themistocles had already built a new city at Piraeus, six kilometres away, with a fort, drydocks, fine public buildings and neatly laid out streets. He had tried to persuade the Athenians to abandon their ancient, rambling, smelly town and move to his bright new city. But the Athenians preferred to stay put. Nor would they abandon the holy places of the Acropolis, even after the Persians reduced them to rubble. Following the war, the Athenians began to rebuild and extend their walls. The whole city was enclosed. So was the road to the port. Later Pericles added a third, long wall to defend Piraeus. As long as the walls stood firm, Athens could always be supplied from the sea. As time passed and the Persians failed to return, the allied states stopped providing ships and sailors and paid cash instead. The Athenian fleet got bigger and bigger.

Athens also had a strong trading fleet. In the old days, piracy had been common. Now control of the seas made it safe for Athenian merchants to expand their businesses. Wine, oil, cloth, pottery and works of art, such as marble and bronze statues, were carried all over the known world as far as Russia, India and China. Grain, metals and timber were essential imports. Luxury goods, including gold, ivory, silks, perfumes, incense and spices, were brought overland from the east on mules and camels, and then transported by sea into Piraeus.

As a naval superpower, Athens soon controlled all the seaborne trade in the Aegean. The mainland could not grow enough grain to feed itself and had to buy what it needed from areas around the Black Sea. Athens took a stranglehold on the food supply and charged what prices and customs duties it felt were necessary.

Early in 453 B.C. Pericles had the funds of the League transferred from Delos to Athens. Allied council meetings were abandoned. From now on all decisions were made in Athens. The former alliance had become an Athenian empire. Even though Athens had signed a non-aggression pact with Sparta, Pericles insisted that there was still the threat of invasion. Also he had to keep the sea free of pirates. The truth was he wanted the money to pay for the rebuilding of the Acropolis. He had plans to make Athens the most beautiful city in the world.

The sanctuary of Delos and the colossal statue of Apollo, who was reputed to have been born on the island.

PERICLES ACCUSED

Other changes weakened the alliance still further. Allied armies were placed under the control of Athenian commanders. Coins minted in Athens became the only legal currency. Serious crimes involving Athenians now had to be tried in Athens. Lands were confiscated, and Athenian colonies were established throughout the Aegean. Towns were encouraged to set up democracies. And once a year each town had to send a sacrificial bull and a suit of armour to the great Athenian festival held in honour of the goddess Athena.

Towns that had been forced into the empire complained that they had been enslaved. Many Athenians, too, thought that Pericles' actions were outrageous. He was attacked by comedy writers in the Great Dionysia. His personal life was ridiculed. Even Pericles' eldest son, spread scandal about his father.

Plutarch describes the accusations against Pericles in the Athenian Assembly:

They insisted that he had brought the utmost disgrace on their city by removing the public treasures from Delos and bringing them to Athens; all people must consider it an act of naked tyranny when they saw money they had been forced to contribute to a war wasted by the Athenians in gilding their city, and decorating it with statues and temples that cost thousands of talents, like a harlot decking herself out with jewels.

Pericles knew that ordinary Athenians were enjoying the fruits of their new-found power. He was sure of their support. Plutarch says:

Pericles' answer to the Assembly was that he was not obliged to give the allies any account of how their money was spent. Athens was running the war and keeping the Persians away. 'They don't give us a single horse, nor a soldier, nor a ship,' he said. 'All they give us is money. This money is no longer theirs because they have given it to us: it is ours as long as we supply the services it was supposed to pay for. It's only fair that now we have all the arms and ships we need to fight a war, we should be allowed to spend what is left on public works that will bring honour and glory to our city for all time.'

Nevertheless, the critics could not be silenced. They declared that Pericles had offended Apollo, the guardian of the Delian League, and that one day Apollo would have his revenge on the Athenians.

CHAPTER 11

Rebuilding Athens

After the Persian capture of Athens and the burning of the Acropolis in 480 B.C., the Athenians swore an oath to leave the holy ruins untouched for all time.

Work had begun on a new temple to Athena which the Persians had destroyed. The Assembly ordered that the remains of its columns should be placed on the edge of the Acropolis where they could be seen from the Agora, the city's business centre and market place. Nobody should forget what the city had suffered at enemy hands.

As part of Pericles' plan for his new Athens, the Agora was rebuilt. The city walls and the new town around the harbour were extended. But pride of place went to the restored Acropolis, to be paid for with the money confiscated from the Delian League. The project would provide well-paid work for thousands of artists, craftsmen and labourers. Pericles thought his popularity would last as long as he lived.

THE ACROPOLIS RISES AGAIN

In 447 B.C. work began on the blackened ruins of the Acropolis. Pericles intended to transform the tiny site, no more than 200 by 300 paces, into a wonder. It was to take fifteen years.

The temple to Athena Parthenos (Athena the virgin), known today as the Parthenon, would be the centrepiece of the restored Acropolis. The architects Kallikrates and Ictinus were chosen to design it and supervise its construction. The most brilliant sculptor in the ancient world, Phidias, was put in charge of the temple's decoration and the building of a gold and ivory statue of the goddess, over 12 metres high.

The stone frieze around the central building showed a procession in honour of Athena, led by 192 youthful horsemen, in memory of the soldiers who died at Marathon. Its statues and friezes were painted and gilded in the brightest colours.

In its long history, the Parthenon saw many changes. For a time, it became a Christian church. The Turks used it as a palace and for storing gunpowder, and finally blew it up. Later, Lord Elgin salvaged what was left of the sculptures and brought them to England. Today you can see them in the British Museum in London.

The Erechthion was the Temple of Erechtheus, supposed to be an early ruler and hero of Athens. It was built on the site of a lightning strike, and it contained three holes in the ground where Poseidon was supposed to have stuck his trident. It was dedicated to him, to Athena and to other gods and heroes. The porch has four statues of female figures, rather than the customary columns to support the roof.

The Temple of Athena Nike had a statue of Athena as goddess of victory, and a sculpted frieze showing the defeat of the Persians.

The Propylaea was the huge protective gatehouse through which visitors entered the sacred precincts. It housed yet another massive statue to Athena and also contained a picture gallery.

Inside the sacred area were other temples, shrines, statues, groves, trees and walks. Here many of the religious processions started or finished, festivals began, oaths were sworn and speeches were made.

The renowned sculptor Phidias, commissioned to decorate the Parthenon, puts the finishing touches to his enormous statue of the goddess Athena.

CHAPTER 12

Living in Athens

We can only imagine what fifth-century Athens looked like. Just a few houses have been excavated in the neighbourhood of the city, and these are very similar to those you can find in the Greek countryside today or on the remote Aegean islands. Our information about houses of those times comes from incidental details in histories, plays and poems. For example, Thucydides tells us that when the people who lived in the countryside around Athens were forced by war to move inside the city walls, they took their doors and window shutters with them.

A country house and farm outside Athens, a rural scene that has basically changed little over the centuries.

COUNTRY AND TOWN

Houses in the country were usually built around a central courtyard, entered by a single, strong wooden door. In the courtyard was a stone altar. The walls were often built on stone foundations. Wood was very expensive and only used where really necessary – in houses built on two levels, for example. The main building material was mud brick, and therefore some form of waterproofing would have been needed. Some houses had thatched roofs, others had roofs of tiles. Often one corner was turned into a protective tower where the family could retreat when robbers were about. Around the house would be animal pens, orchards, vegetable gardens and beehives.

Conditions were more cramped in town. The oldest part of Athens was a maze of narrow, filthy, unpaved, unlit streets. It contrasted badly with the newer areas and the magnificent public buildings Pericles was putting up in the Agora and on the Acropolis. Because Athens had been allowed to grow and spread in such a messy way, both Themistocles and Pericles recognized the need for the

A busy street in Athens, showing men and women of different social classes. On the right, water is being drawn from a fountain.

new town at the Piraeus to be carefully planned. Back in the old town, the houses would have been simple but quite comfortable. People had to be fairly well-to-do to live in the city in the first place. But there was little luxury. The men spent most of their time outdoors, anyway.

Nearly all the rooms faced inwards, opening onto the central courtyard and its altar. Solid walls on the street side made the house secure. The single door could be locked and bolted. Larger, richer households followed the same plan, but the door would have a porch, guarded by a slave porter. Above the door would usually be a herm, a stone pillar with the head of the protecting god carved on it. Some houses had a second storey. There would be a kitchen, a room for eating, storerooms and bedrooms. As time passed, dining rooms became bigger and more elaborate. The dinner party, followed by the drinking party, was an important feature of life. The dining room was a place in which to talk and entertain friends. It probably contained the best furniture, and its walls might be painted or covered with embroidered hangings. The women of the household were not allowed in the dining room. They ate in their own quarters.

The women and the female slaves looked after the basic cooking. Flour was ground at home. Cooking utensils were of earthenware or metal. Kitchens had pottery-lined bread ovens and charcoal grills. Some writers suggest that, because the slaughter of animals and the cooking and carving of meat was almost a religious ritual, it had to be done by the men. As a rule, Athenians liked simple food. Only after the time of Pericles did elaborate meals become common. On special occasions, professional cooks would be hired. In any case, there were plenty of snack bars and restaurants where the men could sit, eat and talk.

WATER AND HYGIENE

Water was scarce enough to be precious in Athens, being piped in from springs in the surrounding hills. A few houses had their own tanks for collecting and saving rainwater. But most people had to send their slaves to the public cisterns or buy it from water carriers. Pisistratus had attempted to improve the water supply, laying pipes under the Agora leading to a public fountain. But there was nothing like the sophisticated system of aqueducts and sewers that the later Romans enjoyed.

The Bronze Age inhabitants of Mycenae and Knossos took bathing more seriously than the citizens of Periclean Athens. Not until much later, when the city became part of the Roman empire, did bathing become an obsession. There were only a few public baths and steam baths linked to the sports centres. Inside the houses, large ceramic or stone washbasins

53

able couches on which pairs of guests would lie. The food was placed on small tables nearby. Tables usually had three legs, suggesting that the floors were not level. Beds were either of the box type or framed with webbing and wooden struts to support a mattress. Rich people slept on beds made of expensive hardwoods, often with elaborately carved legs, inlaid with ivory, silver or even gold. As far as we know, there were no cupboards, just chests and boxes of all sizes for storing clothes, food, money and valuables. Baskets, used for storage and shopping, were suspended from the ceiling to keep out mice and rats. Clothes and other objects were also hung from wooden pegs.

Lighting was provided by olive-oil lamps, which must have been smelly. The rich had lamps of bronze or silver, the poor had pottery ones. In the summer, hours of darkness were short. The lamps would be brought in for men who wished to talk or drink the night away. The poor, however, would rise at dawn and go to bed when it got dark. As a rule, Athenian men spent as little time indoors as possible. Life was conducted in the open air.

Women of an Athenian household cook and prepare dinner.

were filled and emptied by hand. Baths could be taken in large, shallow earthenware bowls. There are pictures on vases of people sloshing water over others standing upright in huge bowls or basins.

At the time of Pericles, Athens must have been producing about 80 tonnes of sewage a day. Athenians customarily used chamber pots. There are illustrations of babies sitting on potties. Sewage piled up in cesspits and dung heaps. Slaves, using shovels and carts, were employed to empty and clean them.

FURNITURE AND LIGHTING

Chairs had been common in earlier times, but in Athens they were rare. The master of a wealthy house might have a chair and a footstool, but women and children sat on stools. In the dining room there were large, comfort-

Floor plan of a typical Athenian house, built around a central courtyard.

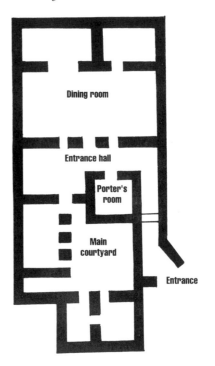

CHAPTER 13

The Athenian Family

Most of what we know regarding life in Athens, and especially the life of women, is very unreliable. What literature has survived, even the great works of history, is written by and concerned with people who were aristocratic or very wealthy men. In the years following Pericles, many such writers were far more interested in the ideals of male beauty and noble minds than in the doings of women. We certainly do not get a realistic picture of everyday life from them. It is said that the philosopher Socrates had a very bad-tempered wife. Putting up with her scolding, said Socrates, made living with other people seem easy. Unfortunately, ordinary people such as cobblers, potters, sailors and slaves did not write their memoirs. We can look at illustrations of them on the vases of the period, but we cannot begin to know what they thought or how they behaved.

MARRIAGE

A man married in his late twenties. His bride would be between thirteen and nineteen and would have had no say in the choice of her husband. The decision rested with the head of the family, usually her father, but if he was dead, with her eldest brother or an uncle. Sometimes the wedding ceremonies would be the first occasion on which the couple actually met. Yet there must have been exceptions. Young people fell in love, and many fathers surely cared enough for their daughters to look after their interests and happiness.

The bride would not be present at the betrothal. Her father would declare before witnesses that he was prepared to give his daughter to the man he had chosen. The bridegroom would promise to support the girl. She would have to be accepted by her

A torchlit wedding procession in Athens. Marriage was an occasion for revelry and song.

husband's extended family or tribe. Only if both parents were born Athenians would their sons have citizens' rights. Except in Sparta, daughters enjoyed few rights and privileges.

There was no public wedding. A private ceremony symbolized the girl's leaving the protection of her father and the gods of his home. She could then be received into the care of her husband and his gods. On the day before the 'wedding', the groom would take holy water from a sacred spring to his wife's home and they would both take a ritual bath. Before doing so, the bride sacrificed her dolls, toys and girdles to Artemis – Apollo's virgin sister. She also cut off her hair, offering it to the goddess, and arranged what was left in a new style. After the bath, the bride's family held a wedding feast. The bride would be there, her face covered by a veil, sitting with her bridesmaids. Her husband to be and his family were not invited.

THE NEW HOME

At sunset, the groom and his friends, who had been having a party of their own, would arrive to claim the girl. At the door of her father's house, the girl might make a symbolic protest at this 'abduction'. Her mother would push her out. Then there would be lots of laughter as the husband and his best friend lifted the bride into a chariot or cart. Singing hymns to Hymen, god of marriage, a crowd of garlanded revellers led the way to the groom's home, carrying torches. The bride's family remained at home, continuing to eat and drink. On the threshold of her new home, the bride was greeted by her mother-in-law.

A ceremony was now held to introduce the wife to the groom's household gods. Instead of confetti and rice, almonds and raisins – symbols of fruitfulness – were thrown at the couple. They then visited the holiest part of the house, the hearth, and sacrificed to Hestia, goddess of homes and families. Two little boys wearing crowns of thistles and oak leaves handed the pair bread in a basket. Only now could the groom lift the veil and look at his wife. He certainly could not kiss her. Kissing in public was considered bad manners. Then the married couple entered the bedroom and shut the door. The people outside would make jokes and would also sing an *epithalamion* – a joyful wedding hymn. A sort of mock porter guarded the bedroom door. It is not clear whether he was symbolically keeping the guests out or keeping the bride in.

On the next day the bride's family and friends arrived with the agreed-upon dowry and the wedding presents. This was an excuse for yet another feast. And it was the first time the two families celebrated together.

THE SPARTAN WEDDING

Most city-states had similar ceremonies. Sparta, as ever, was the exception. It was a military society that believed in educating girls, letting them speak their mind, go out in public, take physical exercise and even run businesses.

In Sparta, which was rather like a huge army camp with no walls, the men lived together in barracks. Although their treatment of women was advanced for their day, they did retain some unusual customs. This is what Plutarch says about their weddings:

Women are married by being abducted. When the bride has been abducted, the bridesmaid takes hold of her and shaves her hair very short. She dresses her in a man's cloak and sandals and leaves her in the bedroom alone in the dark. Then the bridegroom slips quietly into the room. He must not be dead drunk or tired out. He unties her girdle and carries her to bed. After a short time he slips out and goes back to the barracks to sleep with the other young men as usual.

THE WOMAN'S PLACE

All household decisions were made by the head of the family. Domestic, financial and business matters were his affair, and he even did the shopping. He and his sons could roam

A group of privileged young men reclining on couches for a festive meal, attended by a slave.

the house at will, but his wife and daughters usually kept to their own quarters. Certainly they were not allowed into the dining room while guests were there being entertained.

Respectable women might venture out for family occasions, name days, weddings and funerals. They seldom mixed with men in public, although they did have their own choirs and festivals, such as the Thesmophoria in honour of Demeter.

Writers, both ancient and modern, have emphasized the lowly status of Athenian women, who are portrayed as servile, second-class individuals living unhappily in a male

world. They are shown spinning, weaving, making clothes and gossiping. They experimented with cosmetics, perfumes, jewellery and new hairstyles. But they never left the house unless chaperoned and accompanied by slaves. They had no rights and few pleasures. The restrictions imposed on them are similar to those placed on many Muslim women today. There is no evidence that in Athens women complained of their lot. Doubtless there were many unhappy marriages, but

Vase with a picture of a woman spinning, an activity that ancient Greek women were expected to perform.

there must have been others where the wife was loved, respected and consulted by her husband.

Female slaves, country women and the poor had more freedom than their richer city sisters but they had to work hard. Some took jobs as musicians and entertainers. HETAIRAI were rather like Japanese geisha girls. Unlike wives, they were much in demand at parties.

CHILDREN

A wife's main purpose and duty was to have children – preferably boys. A father would wish to pass on the headship of the family to his son so that he might stop work himself and enjoy a happy retirement. Old people were not treated with great respect in Athens. It is said that in the theatre once, an old man was trying to find a seat. The only people who stood to offer him one were the Spartan ambassadors.

When a new baby was a few days old, it was presented to the household gods. For a boy, the house door was decorated with crowns of olive leaves to symbolize wealth and good fortune. For a girl, the crowns were of wool to symbolize a life of housework and child-rearing. The midwife, female relations and slaves who had helped to deliver the child would ritually wash their hands. Then the child was carried to the hearth, where sacrifices were made and the gods asked for their blessing.

A few days later a kind of baptism was held in the home. The first male children were usually named after their fathers and grandfathers. In well-to-do families children were looked after by a nurse who often became a well-loved member of the household.

EDUCATION

In rural areas few children had much schooling. They received basic teaching from their parents and grandparents. Girls learned practical tasks in the women's quarters. Only in Sparta did they get the same start in life as boys. After about 480 B.C., there were schools in Athens for boys from seven to fifteen, but wealthier families employed private tutors. Slaves took the boys to school, carried their books, stayed with them in the classroom, helped with the homework and were thrashed if their charges misbehaved. The pupils learned long sections of the *Odyssey* and the *Iliad* by heart and sang them aloud. They were taught to read and write in ink with a sharp pen on slabs of wood or on wax. Next came music – playing the lyre and singing solo or in the choir. Last and most important was physical education. Running, wrestling, boxing, javelin throwing, jumping, and perhaps horse-riding for the rich, all prepared boys for the arts of war.

There were no public universities or places of higher education. The child of a farmer or craftsman would follow in his father's footsteps. For the sons of richer Athenians, public life beckoned. There were private schools for teaching them to talk, debate, make speeches and understand city politics. But most young men, between the time they left school and joined the army, concentrated on enjoying themselves. The rich chatted, argued, drank and raced horses. They spent much time at the sports centre, exercising and showing off.

SLAVES

Many people in Athens were slaves. Some were born into slavery, others were captured in battle and made slaves. Slaves were bought and sold in the Agora. Even poor families often managed to keep one or two slaves. The city of Athens employed slaves as policemen, as junior civil servants, as silver miners and for a variety of other menial tasks. Building contractors employed them along with freemen. At one shield-making factory in Athens, most of the workers were slaves.

Household slaves probably had a fairly easy time. There was never any suggestion of a slave revolt, as there was often in Sparta and later in Rome. In fact, the Spartans were accused of treating their slaves with great brutality, in order to keep them living in fear. Slaves vastly outnumbered citizens there and revolts could be serious. It was alleged that Spartan boys were encouraged to sneak about at night and beat a few slaves to death just to keep them in their place.

Many Athenians complained that slaves in Athens had far too much freedom and were indulged and spoiled. They never stopped to wonder whether slavery was a good thing or not. Nor would many slaves have given it much thought, since they had no freedom of choice. An Athenian would not have understood what freedom of choice meant.

EARNING A LIVING

The Athenians were mostly farmers. The poor ones worked the land, usually without slaves. The richer ones lived in town on the income from their lands. The land around Athens was poor and often mountainous, so it was easier to raise sheep and goats than grow wheat or barley. Because growing grain was a problem, most of it was imported from the fertile plains of what is now Russia. Olives were the best local crop: the oil was used for cooking and lighting. Much of it was exported. Grapes were cultivated near Athens, but the best wine came from elsewhere. A wide variety of fruit and vegetables was grown. Honey was in great demand and produced in large quantities.

Fish was more readily available than meat. Fishermen used both hooks and nets. As Athens was close to the sea, live fish, lobsters and squid could be transported to the marketplace and kept alive in saltwater tanks. Salted and dried fish were also common.

Hunting was an important source of food rather than a relaxation for the rich. All sorts of game from wild boar to hares and songbirds were trapped, netted or speared.

Almost anything could be bought in the market. Pottery was especially important. Pots were used for storing liquid – wine and olive oil – and for cooking. Decorated tableware tells us more about the lives of Athenians than any other source. The remains of a cobbler's shop have been excavated in the Agora. Sandals were expensive and many people went barefoot. Cloth and clothes were made at home, but expensive fabrics, imported silks and wall hangings could be bought in the Agora. There were also jewellers, silversmiths and goldsmiths, sculptors, carpenters, blacksmiths, armourers, cake and bread shops, snack bars and toy shops.

Vase depicting a realistic scene of women drawing and carrying water.

CHAPTER 14

The End of Pericles

Feeling that the Samian fleet was growing too powerful, Pericles involved the Athenians in a war against the island of Samos. Afterwards he made a speech at the funeral of the young men who had died in the war. Women were allowed to attend state funerals, and some crowned him with garlands, wreaths and thin wool ribbons known as fillets. But the sister of his old rival, Cimon, attacked Pericles. 'This was indeed a famous victory,' she said. 'You certainly deserve these garlands. You have thrown away the lives of these brave citizens, not in a war against our old enemies, the Persians or the Phoenicians, but against a friendly city – one of our allies.'

PRIDE

Pericles grew even prouder. He boasted that it had taken Agamemnon ten years to destroy Troy, but he had destroyed Samos in only nine months. Because they dared not attack Pericles directly, his enemies began to pick on his friends. Phidias, the sculptor, was accused of embezzlement and impiety. People said he had stolen money from the goddess Athena that should have been spent on the Parthenon. The artist was thrown into prison.

Pericles no longer pretended that the Athenian empire was just a friendly alliance. He admitted that it was a tyranny 'which it may have been wrong to acquire, but now is too dangerous to set free'. He said Athens had nothing to fear from the Spartans. But the Spartans could not allow Athens to dominate the Aegean.

Sparta did not rely on Athens for food,

getting its own grain from Sicily. But Athens was even interfering in this part of the Mediterranean. The Spartans urged the Athenians to throw Pericles out, describing him as 'a curse' on his people. The Athenians refused.

As Sparta prepared to attack, Pericles moved all the citizens from the countryside inside the walls that protected the city and its harbour. He knew he could not defeat Sparta on land, but while the port remained free, he believed Athens could hold out forever.

PLAGUE

Because so many people were crowded into the city, conditions became very unhealthy. Soon a plague broke out. More than one-third of the population died. Pericles' two sons, his sister and many other friends and relatives were among the victims. Plutarch said that Pericles did something he had never done before: 'He broke into a weeping and wailing and shed many tears at the funeral of his younger son'. According to Plutarch, too, many people blamed Pericles for the plague because country folk 'had nothing to do but stay penned up like cattle and infect each other with the disease'.

Sophocles' most famous play is *Oedipus Tyrannus*. It was first performed at the Great Dionysia in Athens, possibly in the last year of Pericles' life. At the opening of the play, the city of Thebes, ruled by King Oedipus, is in the grip of a terrible plague. Oedipus sends his brother-in-law, Creon, to Delphi to ask Apollo why the city is being punished. On his return, Creon says:

> There is something corrupt here
> Born and raised on our soil,
>   poisoning our soil,
> Which must be driven away,
>   or it will destroy us.

In the play the corrupt thing is Oedipus himself. Apollo is punishing Thebes for crimes Oedipus has committed, those of murdering his father and marrying his mother. Many in the audience must have thought that Sophocles was inviting them to think about Pericles and his crimes against Apollo.

Pericles was accused in the Assembly of taking bribes, removed from office and given a heavy fine. In 429 B.C. he caught the plague and died in misery, hated by the citizens to whom he had given an empire. They said his pride had brought about his downfall and the ruin of his city.

After Pericles' death, the war dragged on. Athens finally surrendered about twenty years later. The Spartans forced the citizens to destroy their long walls and, for a time, abolished democracy in Athens. But the war had exhausted the Spartans as well. They were conquered by the city of Thebes and eventually absorbed into the Macedonian empire of Philip and his son, Alexander the Great. It was Alexander, who at the age of twenty-six, sat down and cried because there were no more countries left to conquer.

EPILOGUE

When, some 250 years later, Athens became part of the Roman empire, the once-proud city became that empire's centre of learning, culture and philosophy. Roman boys finished their studies in Athens; more than one Roman emperor was initiated into the rites of the goddess Demeter, known as the mysteries of Eleusis; and Athenian architects, builders, sculptors and artists were in demand everywhere. Sadly, however, the fierce pride that had once led them to defy the Persians and build an empire of their own had deserted the creators of democracy.

Athenian refugees flee Athens during the plague that killed Pericles and thousands of his fellow citizens.

Perhaps the greatest memorials to the age of Pericles are the ruins of the Parthenon in Athens and the great masterpieces of classical tragedy: the *Oresteia* of Aeschylus and the Theban plays of Sophocles. The plays were written and performed in ancient Greek, a language no longer spoken today, but they can be brought to life for each new generation by gifted actors. And Apollo's central message in the plays – that man must suffer in order to be wise, and that man grows wise against his will – is as true today as it was then.

Athenian democracy was very different from our own. It did not acknowledge the rights of women, it permitted slavery, and it was open to abuse by cunning men such as Pericles. But it is a concept that has proved sufficiently strong and appealing to have survived through the ages. This ideal was the true legacy of Athens.

Glossary

ACADEMIA   An olive grove outside of Athens, sacred to the hero Academos. The philosopher Plato founded a school there, and the name has led to our words 'academy' and 'academic'.

ACHAEANS   A powerful tribe that dominated the west coast of the Aegean Sea during much of the Bronze Age.

ACROPOLIS   A fortified area in a town where defenders could hold out in a siege.

AEOLIANS   A tribe that may originally have lived on the western mainland but was driven east across the Aegean by invading Dorians.

AGORA   A city centre that was the site of many major public buildings, where most citizens met to talk, relax and do business.

ARCHONS   A small group of city executive officers elected by the Athenians.

AREOPAGUS   The hill in Athens of Ares, the war god, where the council of elders met.

ASSEMBLY   The chief council of Athens. Any Athenian male over the age of eighteen was a member.

CHOREGUS   A person chosen to bear most of the costs of putting on a play at one of the Athenian festivals to honour Dionysus.

DEMES   The ten districts into which the city of Athens was divided for purposes of administration.

DORIANS   A powerful tribe that conquered Peloponnesus.

EPHEBOS   Strictly speaking, a boy eighteen or nineteen years old. More generally, a youth.

FURIES   Female demons who made sure that guilty people were hounded and punished.

HETAIRAI   Women who sang, danced and entertained the guests at all-male drinking parties.

HOPLITE   Infantryman, or foot soldier.

IONIANS   A Peloponnesian tribe believed to have been driven east by the invading Dorians. The Ionians founded a new state in Asia Minor.

LIBATION   A form of sacrifice. At a drinking party or a religious ceremony some wine was poured on the ground as an offering to the gods.

MOTHER EARTH   Ancient fertility goddess.

OBOLS   Small coins worth one-sixth of a drachma each.

OLYMPIANS   The ruling family of gods, headed by Zeus, who lived on Mount Olympus, south of Macedonia. Mount Olympus should not be confused with Olympia, where the Olympic games were held.

ORACLE   The word is given to the place where Apollo resided, or the spirit of wisdom and knowledge that was being consulted, or the words of prophecy delivered by the god's priestess, the Pythia, or Pythoness.

ORCHESTRA   The circular stage in a theatre where the chorus and actors sang and danced.

PHALANX   A military formation in which soldiers advanced shoulder to shoulder in ranks.

TYRANTS   Originally kings; later, kings who exercised brutal power without legal authority.

Index

Numbers in *italics* refer to illustrations.

Academia, 37
Achaeans, 6–8, *6, 8*
Achilles, 26, 38
Acropolis, 15, 22, *23*, 32, 44, 48, 50, 52
Aegean Islands, 7, 16, 52
Aegean Sea, 6–8, 10, 17, 24, 25, 29, 40, 48, 49, 50
Aegeus, 26
Aegisthus, 33
Aeolians, 6–8, 10
Aeschylus, 19, 33, 36–37, 61
Agamemnon, 6, 33, 60
Alexander the Great, 61
Alpheios (river), 40, 42
Altis, grove of, 38, *38*
archon, 36-37, 45
Areopagus (hill), 23
Areopagus (court), 45–47
Argos, 6, 18
Artemisia, 23
Artemisium, 19
Asclepius, 30
Assembly, 16, 17, 44–47, *45*, 49, 50, 61
Assyria, 7
Athens/Athenians, 6–18, *12–13, 14, 15*, 22, 23, *23, 24*, 26, 31–34, *34–35*, 36, 37, 43–50, *44, 47*, 52–61, *52–55, 61*
Attica, 7, 10, 22
Augeas, 38

Babylon, 32
Battles,
    Marathon, 11–14, *12–13, 14*, 16, 17, 19, 27, *28*, 33, 37, 46, 50
    Mycale, 24
    Salamis, 18, 23–24, *24*, 28, 33, 36, 37
    Thermopylae, 19, *22*, 24
Black Sea, 8, 48

Callimachus, 11, 12
China, 48
Cimon, 16, 17, 46–47, *47*, 60
Clytemnestra, 33
Corinth, 40

Creon, 60
Crete, 6, 8
Croesus, 7
Cyclops, 30
Cyclops, The, 34
Cypriots, 19

Daphne, 30
Darius, 7, *9*, 10, 14–15
Dark Ages, 6, *8*
Delian League 48–50
Delos, 25, 29, 48–50, *48–49*
Delphi, *16*, 18, *18*, 22, 24, 25, 28, 29, 30, *30*, 33, 40, 60
democracy, 8, 44-45, 61
Dorians, 6

Ecbatana, 7
Egypt/Egyptians, 7, 8, 15, 19, 33
Elektra, 33
Elgin, Lord, 50
Elis, 38, 40, 41
ephebos, 15
Ephesus, 9
Ephialtes (politician), 46, *47*
Ephialtes (shepherd), 20, 22
Epidaurus, 33
Eretria, 9, 10
Euphranites, 29
Euripides, 33–36

festivals, 31, 36–37,
    Great Dionysia, 36, 49, 60
    Thesmophoria, 57
France, 8
Furies, 33

Gillius, 40
gods and goddesses
    Agraulos, 15
    Ajax, 24, 26
    Apollo, 11, *12, 16–17, 17*–18, 22, *23*, 24–25, 27–30, *29, 30*, 33, 40, 48–49, *48–49*, 56, 60–61
    Ares, 18, 23, 25, 27, 28
    Artemis, 25, 30, 56
    Athena, 22, 24, 33, 41, 49, 50, *50–51*, 60
    Demeter, 25, 29, 38, 43, 57, 61
    Dionysus, 25, 29, 31, 32, 36–37, *34–35*
    Hades, 25, 30, 38
    Hera, 25, 29, 30, 38, 43
    Herakles, 6, 38

Hermes, 25, 30
Hestia, 25, 26, 56
Hymen, 29, 56
Mother Earth, 29, 30, 38
Pan, 25, 30
Poseidon, 23–26, 30, 38, 40, 50
Silenus, 25
Zeus, 17, 25–27, *28*, 29, 30, 38, 40–43
Gorgon, 7

Halicarnassus, 23
Halirrhothius, 23
Herodotus, 9, 19, 21
Hesiod, 32
hetairai, 58
Hippias, 10, 11
Hippodameia, 38, 40, 42
Hippodrome, 42
Hippolytus, 35
Histiaeus, 8–9, *8*
Hittites, 32
Homer, 6, 29, 32
hoplite, 11, *11*, 15, 15
Hyacinthus, 30
Hydarnes, 20

Ictinus, 50
Iliad, 6, 38, 58
Immortals, 19, 20, 22
India, 25, 48
Ion, 46
Ionians, 7, 8, 9, 10, 11, 19, 36
Italy, 8

Kallikrates, 50
Knossos, 6, 53

Lade, 9
Laurium, 17
Leonidas, 19–22, 24
Leotychidas, 24
Leto, 29, 30
Lydia, 7

Macedonia, 61
Malis, 20
Mardonius, 24
Mazda, *20–21*, 24
Medea, 36
Medusa, 7
Menander, 31
Miletus, 8–9, 36
Miltiades, 11–13, *14*, 16, 27, *28*, 46

Mycenae, 6, *6*, 53
Mysteries of Eleusis, 29, 61

Nemea, 40
Niobe, 30

Odysseus, 32
Odyssey, 58
Oedipus, 34, 60–61
Oenomaus, 38, 40, *40*
Olympia, 19, 25, 27, *28*, 38, *38*, 40–43, *41*
Olympic games, 38, 40, 42, 43, *43*
Olympus, Mount, 25, 41
oracle, *16*, 17–18, *23*, 30
Orestes, 33
Oresteia, 61
Orpheus, 29
ostrakon, 47, *47*

Painted Stoa, 16
Parnassus, Mount, 30, *30*
Paros, Parians, 16
Parthenon, *13*, 14, 41, 50, *50–51*, 60, 61
Patroclus, 38
Pausanias (nephew of Leonidas), 24
Pausanias (visitor to Olympia), 41, *41*
Pelopion, 41
Pelops, 38, *38–39*, 40, *40*, 42, 43
Pentheus, 35
Pericles, 6, 14, 16, 17, 22, 25, 28, 31, 33, 36, 37, 41, 42, 43, 44–50, *44*, *45*, *47*, 52, 53, 54, 55, 60–61, *61*
Persephone, 29, 38
Perseus, 7
Persia/Persians, 7, 8, 9, 10–14, *12–13*, 16–24, *23*,

24, 36, 37, 44, 46, 48, 49, 50, 60, 61
phalanx, 15
Phaleron, 11, 12, 13
Pheidippides, *see* Philippides
Phidias, 41, *50–51*, 60
Philip of Macedon, 61
Philippides, *10*, 11, 13, 14
Phocians, 19, 20
Phoenicians, 19, 23, 60
Phrynichus, 36
Piraeus, 48, 53
Pisa, 38, 40
Pisistratus, 32, 53
Plataea/Plataeans, 11, 12, 14, 24
Plutarch, 28, 44, 49, 56, 60
Pnyx hill, 45, *45*
Precinct of Herakles 13
priests, 26
Propylaea, 50
Prytaneion, 42
Pylades, 19
Pylos, 6
Pythia, *16*, 18,
Python, 29, *30*
religion, 25–30

Rhodes, 8
Rome/Romans, 6, 33, 42, 53, 59, 61
Russia, 8, 48, 59

sacrifice, *26–27*, 28–29, 37
Samos/Samians, 60
Sandauce, 28
Sardis, 9, *9*, 19, *20–21*, 24
seers, 26, 28
Segesta, *25*, *33*
Sicily, 8, *25*, *33*, 37, 42, 60
Silenus, 25
slaves, 54, 55, 57, *57*, 58, 59

Socrates, 55
Sophocles, 33, *36*, 37, 60, 61
Spain, 8
Sparta/Spartans, 6, 7, *6–7*, 9, *10*, 11, 13, 17, 18, 19–22, *19*, 24, 30, 42, 45, 46–47, 48, 56, 58, 59, 60, 61
Sumeria, 32
Syria, 8

Tantalus, 38
Temple
    of Apollo, *18*
    of Athena Nike, 50
    of Athena Parthenos, 50
    of Hera, 41
    of Zeus, 25, 41, 43
Thebes/Thebans, 6, 19–22, 34, 60–61
Themistocles, 17, 28–29, 48, 52
Theseus, 26, 36
Thespians, 19, 20
Thespis, 32
Thrace, 7
Thucydides, 44, 46, 52
Tiryns, 6
Troy, 6, *6*, 26, 30, 32, 33, 60
Turkey, 8, 50
tyrants, 8, 32

Ukraine, 8

Xanthippus, 16, 17, 22, 36
Xerxes, 15, 17, 19–20, 22–24, *20–21*, *22*, 28

Zephyrus, 30
Zeus, *see* gods and goddesses
Zeus, Altar of, 41, 43, *41*